D0357381

TRUSTING GOD

TRUSTING GOD

Christian Faith in an Age of Uncertainty

EARL F. PALMER

REGENT COLLEGE PUBLISHING
Vancouver, British Columbia

Trusting God
Copyright © 2006 Earl F. Palmer
All rights reserved.

Published 2006 by Regent College Publishing
5800 University Boulevard, Vancouver, BC V6T 2E4 Canada
Web: www.regentpublishing.com
E-mail: info@regentpublishing.com

Unless otherwise noted, Scripture quotations are from Today's
New International Version of the Bible, copyright © 2001,
2005 by the International Bible Society. Used by permission of
Zondervan Publishers.

The author and publisher gratefully acknowledge permission
to quote *Telephone Poles and Other Poems* by John Updike.
Used by permission of Alfred A. Knopf, Inc.
Copyright © 1961 by John Updike.

Regent College Publishing is an imprint of the Regent
Bookstore <www.regentbookstore.com>. Views expressed in
works published by Regent College Publishing are those of the
author and do not necessarily represent the official position of
Regent College <www.regent-college.edu>.

Library and Archives Canada Cataloguing in Publication Data

Palmer, Earl F
Trusting God : Christian faith in an age of uncertainty /
Earl F. Palmer.

Includes bibliographical references.
ISBN 1-57383-329-0

1. Faith. 2. Christian life—Presbyterian authors. I. Title.

BT771.3.P34 2006   234'.23   C2005-905654-1

CONTENTS

For our grandchildren who have already been my teachers in the meanings of faith, hope and love:

Sarah Alaina and Emily Grace Welsh
Andrew Jonathan and Thomas Christian Palmer
Katherine Elizabeth, Peter Olav and Emma Anne Jacobsen

And for two beloved friends who have taught our family the meanings of faith, hope and love:

Julie and Vincente Sayson

ACKNOWLEDGMENTS

I want to thank the students at First Presbyterian Church of Berkeley and New College Berkeley who first studied with me these themes of faith and doubt. The Wednesday evening classes here at UPC also helped me to see the importance of a careful exploration of faith in a time of uncertainty.

Our own family members, Anne, Jon, and Elizabeth, and their spouses, Greg, Kara Diane, and Eric, have also been encouragers to me. Our grandchildren are now teachers of mine in all matters and in this grand theme as well: Sarah, Katherine, Andrew, Peter, Tommy, Emma, and our littlest—Emily. Jon's study of Job when he was an undergraduate at college was especially influential in helping me to see and understand the crisis of faith in the book of Job.

To Shirley, my wife, I owe special gratitude for the supportive loyalty and love that has been the beautiful grace-faith glue in our family.

I am very grateful to my editor at Regent College Publishing, Rob Clements, for his counsel and encouragement. Also to my

Executive Assistant, Nancy Schuldt for her help in this project and our Learning Resources Coordinator here at University Presbyterian Church, Sue Dryer for her editorial guidance. Special thanks also to one of our family photographers, Kara Diane, for the cover photo of my grandson, Andrew, and his kite.

As I write these words, many friends young and old come to my mind because they have allowed me to share in different ways in their journeys of the thousand and single steps toward faith.

I wish them well. —E. F. P.

SUCH A WINDY PLACE

Such a windy place
To find the water and food that will
Last and give me time while dust
And leaves, ideas and words blow constantly in my face

How can I pause and think
　　　wonder and ask
　　　decide and do
　　　in such a windy place

It takes a Good Shepherd with skill and will
　　　who loves his sheep on a thousand hills
while we pause and think
　　　wonder and ask
　　　decide and do
in such a windy place

—Earl F. Palmer

(A poem in honor of the 25th Anniversary of New College, Berkeley)

1

FIRST AND SECOND THOUGHTS

Matthew 21:28-32

One of the shortest parables Jesus told is about two brothers:

> "What do you think? A man had two sons; and he went to the first and said, 'Son, go and work in the vineyard today.' And he answered, 'I will not'; but afterward he repented and went. And he went to the second and said the same; and he answered, 'I go, sir' but did not go." (Matthew 21:28-30)[1]

Jesus told this story on the Monday of Holy Week to a very nervous crowd. He followed up the brief parable with a question: "Which of the two did the will of his father?" (v. 31). His listeners replied with their answer that the first son did the will of the father; then Jesus addressed the people with salty words. His words were stern but there is good news hidden in them:

> "Truly, I say to you, the tax collectors and the harlots go into the kingdom of God before you. For John came to you in the way of

righteousness, and you did not believe him, but the tax collectors and harlots believed him; and even when you saw it, you did not afterward repent and believe him." (Matthew 21:31-32)

How are we to understand this incident with its parable and statement? We begin by trying to understand the parable itself as a short story. The parable is brief but it is powerfully suggestive. What makes the story work as a story is that each son has a fault.

The first one too hastily opposes his father's will as if it were against him. He comes across to us as independent and defiant; he rejects the morning work suggestions of his father and stalks out of the house, determined to do what he wants to do instead of what his father had requested. But later on, his father's will makes sense to him and he does go to work in the vineyard. This son might be described as a son one who is a big problem at breakfast, but a joy at supper.

The second son in this short story is different from the first. He avoids conflict with his father; he says what he thinks his father wants to hear. But he does not go to work in the vineyard. His warm and cheerful agreement in the morning was an encouragement to the family still in shock from the rude hostility of the first son. But as afternoon wore on, it became clear that this second son—for whatever reasons—never showed up for work in the vineyard. He could be described as a joy at breakfast but a big problem at supper. Unfortunately for all such folk this is a supper parable not a breakfast parable.

AN UNDERSTANDING OF HUMAN PERSONALITY

What is Jesus teaching in this parable?

First of all, here, as in all of his parables, Jesus shows that he really understands human personality. Just as agricultural

14

parables of Jesus are agriculturally accurate, so the interpersonal parables are psychologically accurate. Jesus shows by means of this parable that he fully expects sharp and even negative reactions to the kingly claims of his Lordship upon our lives.

This is a Kingdom parable in which the story has to do with the claim that is being made by the father toward two sons. That call is definite and the stakes are important. Therefore, the Storyteller is not surprised that the first son should resist the call to discipleship upon his life. By the way he tells the story, Jesus shows his awareness of the intense and conflicting pressures that are focused upon those moments in which a human being discovers the discipleship implications of the Lord's reign upon his or her life.

The parable also shows that Jesus expects the evasive and slippery response that comes from the second son. The teacher is neither surprised by the struggle of the rebel son nor by the temporary or even the possibly staged agreement of the apparent compliance of the second son. Jesus' portrayal of the struggling son is very encouraging to all of us who have experienced the struggle of our will with the commands of the law and the gospel. Jesus' portrayal of the evasive son may not be as encouraging for us to hear but it is equally important for us. Both portrayals keep the record straight.

In the New Testament there are different kinds of parables. Some are examples drawn from agricultural or daily living experiences (such as the mustard seed example that Jesus gives in Matthew 13:31-32). Other parables are stories about interpersonal relationships and human reactions.

This parable of the two sons is the second kind of parable. This means that Jesus has woven into the story two thematic threads present in all good stories—one comic and the other tragic. Together they produce what C.S. Lewis once described as a "sudden perception of incongruity."

The comic line here is represented by the first son who, in spite of strong protests of youthful fury, does in fact surprise the whole family when he finally settles down and goes to work in the vineyard. "What a surprise we all had from that boy. We never thought he would amount to anything!"

The tragic line is represented by the second son who misses out on everything important represented by the vineyard as the kingdom of God. His studied and polished agreeability at early morning cheated him from the chance to really meet his father. Would it not have been better had he argued with his dad as had the first son? An honest family argument at least causes people to get to know what each person is like and how each one thinks.

The second son's compliance might have been a device for avoidance, and it worked too well. He also missed out on the clarifying experience of repentance. The stormy first son goes through the journey of working through his impetuous early defiance and then changing his mind. The second son avoided all of that by a too early and too easy endorsement of the father's point of view. He had never really thought about the matter because he only said "yes" to get away quickly from the place where decisions are made.

Finally, this son also misses out on the goal for his whole existence—the vineyard of God for which all of life is intended.

A Definition of Faith

The principal teaching of Jesus' parable has to do with the word *faith* itself. Jesus decides to interpret only one theme from this story of the two sons, and he imprints that one theme upon the parable by the question he asks of his listeners: "Which of the two did the will of his father?" *The one who did the will of the father is the one who trusted the father*—even though it took until the afternoon for him to do it.

This parable defines faith in a stormy and exciting way: Faith is the mixture of hearing *and* doing the will of God. Therefore, we can correctly describe this parable as a parable about the meaning of faith—*pisteuo*, in the original Greek of the New Testament. This same word is also translated as "believe" or "have faith."

Jesus speaks in the language of faith as he makes his challenge to the crowd. He scolds those apparently devout leaders who did not obey the "way of righteousness" that God had spoken to them through his prophet, John the Baptist. "And you did not *believe* him, but the tax collectors and the harlots *believed* him; and even when you saw it you did not afterward repent and *believe* him" (Matt. 21:32, italics added). Notice how Jesus repeats "have faith (in)" or "believe" three times.

Finally, the parable makes a whimsical point in the story of the first son. The parable shows that, to quote C. S. Lewis once again, "second thoughts are better than first thoughts." At first, this son was so sure that his father's will was all wrong. But the longer he thought about the matter, the more sense it made to him and, finally, by the afternoon it became clear to him that his father's will had indeed made good sense. The father's will had worn well as the day progressed.

The Examination of Faith

In the way Jesus describes it, faith in God benefits from the stormy, honest, vigorous examination of every possibility. Given some time and the chance to think it over, the first son decided in favor of doing his father's will. C. S. Lewis captures this element of durability in his discussion of the radical center of faith and its most basic source—the durability of Jesus Christ himself. Commenting on the "Grand Miracle" of the Incarnation, Lewis points out that the good news about Jesus Christ lacks the "obvious attraction" of pessimism, optimism, pantheism and materialism. Initially, each of these seems confirmed by "multitudes of facts," but in time each encounters "insuperable obstacles." The credibility of the Incarnation of Jesus Christ does not lie in its obviousness but in its intellectual durability. Jesus Christ makes more sense as the day moves from morning to afternoon. As Lewis puts it, "Its hour comes when these wholesale creeds have begun to fail us."[2]

The parable teaches us that it is better to finally believe what at first you cannot say than to say at first what you don't believe.

Faith in God is not meant to be a simple matter, and the parable of the two sons makes that fact clear. In a very few words, Jesus has set in motion some of most complicated questions and possibilities about the real meaning of faith. From Jesus' story we now know that human freedom in deciding is not taken lightly by the One who is the storyteller of this parable. Jesus himself preserves for us the lag time needed between hearing the call to discipleship and our decision to actually trust the Lord of the call.

The parable also stands like a warning sign against the "easy-street" speeches we human beings are tempted to put in place of the harder and longer-lasting way of the disciples' faith. This story tells us about the struggle that is involved as we decide what we really are going to do about God's will for his vineyard and his people. That choice is usually not an uncomplicated decision, and Jesus, by telling the story of the two sons, preserves the complicated nature of all decision making while at the same time, he encourages us to act in favor of God's will.

What I want to do in this book is to examine the ingredients that come together in that deciding event of the two brothers. How do the claims of Jesus Christ become persuasive to a person in our century against such contemporary competitors as pantheism, materialism, optimism, and pessimism? Some people I meet are sure they have no problems they cannot handle by themselves; they have no need for the Father's vineyard, nor does their world. They are *optimists* in a classical religious sense—self-contained and inner oriented. They feel positive about the future of their own private kingdom.

When I was an undergraduate at the University of California, Berkeley, I remember standing one afternoon at the corner of Bancroft and College Avenue with a friend who lived in the same co-op as I. He had been observing with alarm my journey of faith and my involvement in the dorm Bible study and the church college group. We were standing next to a telephone pole and he was sternly warning me about what he considered to be the dangers of my slide into religious foolishness.

He spoke with great urgency, "The trouble with Christians is that you depend too much on God when you should depend more on yourself; why do you need that crutch? Religious fanatics really make me furious!" And with that final statement, he hit his fist full force into the telephone pole. This was before the days of karate and kung fu hands of iron. His face winced, but he carried on as if everything were the same, because he was a philosophical optimist who needed nothing beyond his own resources.

I don't remember much more of the verbal part of that particular encounter, but his desperate emotional unraveling demonstrated to me the philosophical and psychological inadequacy of his self-contained classical optimism. What I realized that afternoon was that my friend was the fanatic, and I hoped for his sake that sooner or later his own myth of self-reliance would hurt as badly as his hand. Optimism as a religious-philosophical-psychological worldview is a very dangerous fanaticism because it does not ask enough hard questions and is too quickly impressed by its own symbols of power.

Prince Andre in Leo Tolstoy's *War and Peace* is an idealistic optimist, and his powerful hero is Napoleon, just the kind of self-assured and successful man that Andre himself wanted to be. But a moment came when everything changed for the young Russian soldier. It happened on the battlefield as Andre lay wounded and the hero of his life came into view. It was Napoleon himself, making an inspection of the prisoners of the battle.

Andre is surprised by how small Napoleon looked as the emperor stood at the midpoint between dead and dying prisoners and the cloudy sky. It was the larger criteria of Andre's dead comrades and of the possibility of his own death that created a new crisis for Andre. His Napoleonic worldview, with its idealism of power, collapsed at the very moment when he was so sure it would mean the most to him—the moment when he saw the great emperor in person, but he noticed the vast dimensions of the sky beyond Napoleon's face that now seemed small and irrelevant.

My friend at the telephone pole may not have been an optimist at all. Perhaps he was at bottom a pessimist who was certain that in the end everything was badly and permanently injured, which is why he was preoccupied with crutches and why he put up with the intense physical pain of his hand impacting against the telephone pole. Pessimism has already decided that there is no help and, therefore, it accuses with rage all affirmations of hope. But in the end pessimism has nothing to offer but its warnings.

I have also wondered if his objection may have been, at least in part, a pantheist objection. Pantheism has focused its attention upon the inner divine consciousness of the human being, and therefore is offended by the claim of the Christian gospel that God is the one who is able and who must speak for himself. Perhaps this is what bothered him about my weekly exposure to Bible studies, because he could see that the more I read the Bible the less I saw myself as a god.

Materialism is also a strong possibility; like the pantheist, a materialist chooses an object for worship, a concrete center point which shall be for that person the center of focus. Therefore, the very possibility that God is *extra nos* (outside ourselves) and hence able to make his own character known within human history, and on his own terms, is rejected because that it is a very dangerous possibility for both the person who has already decided that divine reality is contained within the highly spiritual inner consciousness of the human self, as well as for the person who is trying to find meaning in the concrete opportunities and gifts of the historical necessity of materialism.

But one thing I have learned is that whatever faith is, it must make sense within the strongly contested places for deciding, like the two brothers of the parable, so that we can live with them into the afternoon. Faith must be able to make sense in the time lag between hearing and doing; between the time I hear Jesus Christ and the moment I decide to trust Jesus Christ.

QUESTIONS FOR FURTHER STUDY

1. Can you think of some reasons why the first son would not want to do the father's will?

2. Can you think of reasons that caused the second son to fail to go to the vineyard after he said yes?

3. What do you think are some reasons why Jesus told this parable?

4. Did you learn something about faith from this parable?

2

FAITH IS AN AMEN WORD

Romans 1:16-17

The question "Who do you believe in?" is a more fundamental question than "How do you believe?" The dynamics involved in how we may believe are important to consider, but not at all as important as the larger question; and that has to do with the object of our belief. This distinction has always been true in the sciences and it is just as true in interpersonal decision-making or in deciding upon ultimate values. When it comes to science, even the most hesitating and tentative confidence in an accurate hypothesis is better than bold and unreserved trust in a faulty hypothesis. The penalty in the first instance is a slowdown in the experience of the results in the research project; but the penalty in the second instance is the disaster of blind alleyways and false conclusions.

In other words, the most vital key to a positive result in the scientific research is truth, not enthusiasm. The zeal and hard work of a persistent scholar is very important to the final breakthrough of the research project; but still the most important fact is the truthfulness of the collection of hypotheses and the evidences upon which the experiment is being constructed.

This principle is applicable in athletics as well. Races are not won without heart and desire, nor are they won without a basic respect for the truth requirement of the sports event. There are certain truths of the event that must be followed in terms of speed, balance, angles of approach and the hard, steady work of physical conditioning.

For the athlete to have a winning performance, for a pole vaulter to reach 18 feet in world competition or for a diver to execute a backward three and one-half dive, each must obey the truth requirements of their respective events. The competitor must trust those truths and entrust himself or herself to those truths of the event in order to realistically compete. And this is where the strong desire of hard work and intensity of will mixes with truth to create a record-breaking jump or dive.

I have met people who want so much to believe that they put their faith in the very act of believing itself; they have faith in faith. These are people who are easily taken advantage of in every enterprise. But what is then described as "faith" is not faith in the Christian sense of the word anymore than such a desperate confidence in the need to be able to say something for sure is responsible scientifically, interpersonally or politically.

WHAT, THEN, IS FAITH?

The earliest word in the Bible for faith is a word from the Old Testament so treasured by the people of the sacred Scriptures that they preserved it into the Greek New Testament in its original Hebrew form. It is the word *Amen.* This word (*AMN* in its root form) is so ancient that philologists cannot find other language group sources to aid us in establishing its earliest meanings. We must watch its extensive use in the Old Testament in order to fully appreciate all that it means.

In its most generic sense it is used to describe the foundation stones of the Temple, as in 2 Kings 18:16. It means "sure peg" in Isaiah 22:22-23. It also means "lasting" or "continual," as in Deuteronomy 28:59. When a Hebrew man or woman heard the various words derived from the root *AMN* the basic idea that came to his or her mind was that of "constancy."[1] In the Old Testament, when this word refers to God it means "faithful" (see Deut. 7:9; Isa. 49:7; Jer. 42:5), and when it refers to persons it means "faith" (Neh. 9:8).

Amen is the word commonly used in reference to the promises of God (Ps. 89:19; Isa. 55:3) and to human response to God's faithful promises and his mighty acts (Exod. 4:31; Ps. 106:12; Gen. 15:6).

All of this means that the Amen theology of faith is clearly framed for us in the Old Testament. Human faith in the Bible means "putting down our weight upon the faithfulness of God." Faith, therefore, is our response to the evidence of God's self-evidence. In Hebrew, "to have faith" literally means to make secure in God.[2]

Therefore, *Amen* is used in a double way throughout the Bible. When it refers to God and his promises it means "faithful" or "faithfulness"; when it refers to our act it means "faith." This double use is dramatically present in Psalm 41:13: "Blessed be the LORD, the God of Israel, from everlasting to everlasting! Amen and Amen." The final words of this psalm could be interpreted "God's faithfulness for our faith."

Our Lord began many of his speeches in the same way, and he intended the same meaning: "Amen, Amen, I say unto you . . . ."

He is announcing to his listeners, "This is a faithful saying and, therefore, you may rightly put your trust in my words."

FAITH IS OUR RESPONSE TO EVIDENCE

Biblical belief, therefore, is not our faith in our ability to have faith, it is our faith in the faithfulness of God; it is our response to the evidence we discover of God's trustworthiness.

In his letter to the Romans, the Apostle Paul makes use of a double quotation of the word "faith": "For I am not ashamed of the gospel:... in it the righteousness of God is revealed through faith for faith" (Rom 1:16-17). We can recognize in this double use of the Greek word for "believe" the rich underpinnings of the Amen theology of the Old Testament. Paul is telling the Romans that God's faithfulness deserves our faith.

Faith, therefore, is not a leap of suspended judgment that plants our feet squarely in the air; nor is it based upon a bold confidence in fragile evidence.[3] Faith in the Bible is our response to evidence, and this is why the question of what it is we are asked to believe in is of such central importance to the Christian. The greatest creeds of Christian faith have always focused primarily upon the source of faith itself rather than upon the means of faith.

Karl Barth makes the following observations concerning the earliest ecumenical Christian creed, the Apostles' Creed.

> It is noteworthy that, apart from the first expression 'I believe' the confession is silent upon the subjective fact of faith. Nor was it a good time when this relationship was reversed, when Christians grew eloquent over their action, over the uplift and emotion of the experience of this thing, which took place in man, and when they became speechless as to what we may believe.[4]

Faith is not an art form or a skill that is developed by the mastery of techniques of believing, even though faith is a dynamic and growing experience that benefits from every exercise in faith. What is most basic, however, is that our growth in faith is not a growth in the methods of trusting but it is growth in our confidence in the character of God. This is the good news about faith, but ironically it is good news we sometimes resist because we may desire more exotic belief formulas.

The Old Testament-New Testament Amen theology of faith was too uncomplicated for the first- and second-century Gnostics who wanted much more interesting formulas and mysteries of "spiritual" breakthrough. For them the methods of believing were all-important and involved secrets to be learned and methods of spiritual awareness to be mastered. It was gnosticism that created the heresies of faith just as legalism created heresies of works. They borrowed from Plato's insistence upon the distinction between appearance and reality and, from that standpoint, it was then possible to establish a religious elite of persons who were especially tuned toward spiritual reality and who had learned the secrets of progress into the deeper mysteries.

Notice that what has happened in such an instance is that the eyes of the believer who became caught up in Gnostic presuppositions have been turned away from Jesus Christ and his sufficient grace toward the methods of the spiritual apprehension of inner secrets and special knowledge (*gnosis*). Faith now becomes a skillful mastery of a few religious geniuses who are able to probe behind and beyond the straightforward Amen faithfulness of God's character as revealed in the law and the gospel and therefore complete and adequate in Jesus Christ as Savior and Lord. The methods of the knowing of the way become more important than the Lord of the way.

Both the Old and New Testaments oppose this false emphasis upon faith that is too preoccupied with its own progress. Therefore, from the Bible's standpoint, the true secret of faith is its object, not its technique. This is the significance of our Lord's double use of the word "Amen".

Hudson Taylor the founder of the Overseas Missionary Fellowship, described his own spiritual secret as his growing confidence in the faithfulness of God. There we have a non-gnostic description of faith. The secret is not Taylor's courage or his obedience or his spiritual mastery of steps toward maturity. The secret for him is God's gracious character and nothing else. Whatever else we want to say about faith and the dynamics of believing, we must not try to go beyond this fundamental Amen of biblical faith—as if there were secrets greater than what God has already revealed by his promises fulfilled in his son.

The Gnostic heresy is the heresy that Dr. Dale Bruner describes as the heresy of *hyper-* (Greek for "more").

> The Corinthians' preoccupation with what they understood as spiritual, namely the remarkable and powerful, lifted them above (*hyper*) both the Spirit's corporate and individual spheres of action: specifically above the common lot of believers in the Church. . . . In a word, Paul wants to turn the eyes of the Corinthians from the spirit of *hyper* which boasts, to the spirit of *agape* which builds . . . . The crucified Christ himself is this way's classic content.[5]

It is about Jesus Christ and his grace and trustworthiness not "our" journey of faith. He is the constant and we are the variable. It is not so bad to be the variable if Jesus of Nazareth is the constant.

God has already shown us enough, and it is this evidence of his faithfulness and love in which we trust in when we believe.

Make a joyful noise to the Lord, all the lands!
Serve the Lord with gladness!
Come into his presence with singing!
Know that the Lord is God!
It is he that made us and we are his;
we are his people,
the sheep of his pasture.
Enter his gates with thanksgiving,
and his courts with praise!
Give thanks to him, bless his name!
For the Lord is good;
his steadfast love endures forever,
and his faithfulness to all generations. (Psalm 100)

One afternoon, the late Dr. Henrietta Mears, the founder of Forest Home Christian Conference Center, and who for many years was on the staff of Hollywood Presbyterian Church, shared with several of us who were young pastors about the discoveries she had made during her life as a Christian. Someone asked her if she would have done anything differently if she could travel the same journey again. I remember that I thought the question rude but her reply was wonderful.

Miss Mears said, without a moment to think about the question, "I would trust God more." Here is wise and good counsel of a person who is sharing with young friends the discovery she had made about the love and faithfulness of her Lord. She had found him to be completely trustworthy; therefore, the focus is upon the Shepherd-Lord of her faith journey, not upon the methods of her journey.

Put more of your weight upon the faithfulness of God. How can we do that? Only as we discover how substantial and trustworthy he is.

IT BEGINS WITH AMEN

Now we can understand the fundamental difference between Christian biblical theology and Christian existential philosophy. The latter begins from my present living context and works back to find convictions and meanings that will make sense to the experiences I am having here and now. This is the approach of the post-modern Christian existential philosophy with its emphasis upon present experiences and the narratives of our present existence situations as the beginning point.

Christian biblical theology has as its working premise a different beginning point. It starts with the prior revelation of God's character, the speech of self disclosure that God has already revealed in Holy Scripture, and then works forward from that starting point toward the present existence questions and situations. It begins with "Amen" and then seeks to work through the implications of God's revealed will toward the real present in which we live today.

Helmut Thielicke puts it this way in his *Theological Ethics:* "The philosopher, for all the weight of tradition, begins fundamentally with himself . . . the theologian refers back to the historical realities which determine the path . . . namely, Scripture and the fathers."[6]

Later in his discussion, Professor Thielicke makes the distinction between Paul Tillich as an example of the philosophical-theological approach and the Barmen Declaration as an example of the biblical-theological approach. At the Synod in Barmen, Germany, May 29-31, 1934, Christians met together who were deeply caught up in the situational crisis of Naziism and they wanted to stand responsibly as Christians in the face of its danger to the world and to the gospel.

> Yet despite the urgency of the situation which called it forth,
> the Declaration begins not with an analysis of the situation but
> with the backward reference . . . each of its six articles begins
> with the text of Scripture. Only in the process of expounding
> these texts does the Synod arrive at a diagnosis of the totalitar-
> ian state and course of action for the believing community.

Tillich stands in contrast to the Barmen theological approach, and primarily to its chief writer Karl Barth. As a Christian philosopher, Tillich has a twentieth-century beginning point so that his "theology is so constructed that he first analyzes the present situation in terms of a question inherent in the situation itself and then looks for a relevant Christian answer."[7]

It seems to me that we, as Christian thinkers, want to do both kinds of enquiry. But the most important of the two is that study which begins with the truth God has revealed and moves toward the particular life situations from the standpoint of that revealed truth.

A young married man called me a few years ago on the phone to ask some advice. From his conversation, I learned of a serious misunderstanding and difference of opinion between him and his wife that was creating tremendous stress in their marriage. I asked him if either of them went to church or were involved in any kind of Christian fellowship, since they both had come from active Christian backgrounds. He said that since they had arrived in the San Francisco Bay area they had no contact with any Christians or Christian fellowship.

Here was a case of two young adults who had no input into their life together as a married couple except from each other, some shared recreational interests, and of course, their clash of opinion over the issues of their misunderstanding. In my opinion, what they needed was some input that was basic and good and fresh in itself. They needed input that was not tied into their problem. This is why, though I recommended a marriage counseling experience for them, I certainly did not recommend that they now find some theological group that will "help you in your problem." They needed to go much further back than that and discover truth about God and his faithfulness that is much more basic than the particular problem this couple is trying to solve. I urged them to read the Bible together, worship God together, and find the sources of hope before they would try to find the solutions to the problems.

It is a little bit like the strategy in football. First, a wide receiver needs to run to the place near where the ball is to be thrown by the quarterback before he starts looking for the ball. Some people look for the ball too soon. First they need to learn the plays, then their formation in the line, and then to run to the place called for in the play.

The fact that Jesus Christ is Lord is a much more basic fact than that he answers the problems we have in everyday living. It seems to me that we should start with the "Amen" facts about God and work forward toward the everyday experiences of our every day. This is the most relevant course to take.

QUESTIONS FOR FURTHER STUDY

1. In Romans 1:16-17, Paul uses the words "faith for faith." What do you think Paul means by this double use of the word *faith*?

2. Why is it that Paul is not ashamed of the "gospel"?

3. How do you react to the following sentence: "What we believe in is more important than how we believe"?

3

FAITH IS A
FREEDOM WORD

Deuteronomy 6:1-9

Faith is a freedom word! Not only is the God of the Bible free, but God has, in his own sovereignty, made the decision that grants to us the dominion of freedom as well. We may track that decision by God in the earliest narratives of Genesis and throughout the whole of the Bible into the final scenes of the book of Revelation. Adam and Eve are free to name the animals; it is in this dominion that science is born with all of the research and invention possibilities that emerge from the freedom to name and classify data. God further honors men and women by calling the animals by the names we choose. The real freedom granted to man or woman is moral as well as scientific; it means that we are free to choose for or against God's will. Cain and Abel are free to worship, but the tragic side of that freedom is that Cain is also free to choose to murder.

One way to understand the narrative of Israel's history is to see it as a journey of choices. It is a journey of choices made by people—kings and prophets, both good and bad—and the story is about the consequences that result from those choices. It is the subjective freedom thread that runs through the book of Psalms and the prophets with such powerful intensity. We see that subjectiveness (subjectivity) in the words of David: "The Lord is my light and my salvation; whom shall I fear?" (Ps 27:1). When David praises God or complains or asks for help, what he says shows not only his feelings but also the decisions he has made: "O LORD, rebuke me not in thy anger . . . There is no soundness in my flesh . . . Lord, all my longing is known to thee, my sighing is not hidden from thee" (Ps. 38:1,3,9 KJV).

The New Testament reveals the same subjective richness. By his parables, Jesus calls out to his listeners to respond with our own feelings and choices: "He who has ears to hear, let him hear" (Matt. 11:15; 13:9, 43; Mark 4:9,23; and others). The choices are our own and no one can make them for us. When Paul urges the Romans to "present your bodies" (Rom. 12:1), he acknowledges that faith is our act and our critical moment—no one else can present my body or yours in gratitude to God's grace. The seven letters that begin the last book of the Bible have the same inescapable personal call to response: "Behold, I stand at the door and knock; if any one hears my voice and opens the door, I will come in and eat with him, and he with me" (Rev. 3:20).

THE SUBJECTIVE NATURE OF FAITH

We who live in the twenty-first century are also free, free to trust in God, free to doubt or to wonder about God. The possibilities are complicated and, because of these possibilities, every exploration of the meanings of faith and believing must consider the subjective nature of faith. Faith in the Bible not only has to do with its source and object (God), it also has to do with the mind, the heart, and the will of the man or woman who believes and doubts and wonders why.

The subjective language of faith is expressed by many words throughout the Bible, but I think the most expressive and important of these is the Hebrew word *shama,* which is used in various forms and settings some 1,050 times throughout the Old Testament. Its most famous usage is found in Deuteronomy 6: "Hear [*shama*], O Israel, The LORD our God, the LORD is one. Love the LORD your God with all your heart and with all your soul and with all your strength." *Shama* means "to hear" and "to obey." In Genesis 11:7 it also means "to understand." It means "to agree and make our own mind up about what we see and recognize to be true." That indeed is faith.

Faith acts upon discovery and dares to test out the implications of that discovery. Crisis words like "repent" and worship words like "bow," the words of "praise" and "thanksgiving" are examples of the subjective language of faith. Each of these words expresses personal response to God. Such vocabulary describes the intensity of the struggle and the stresses of decision-making, as well as the words of resolution.

Faith is not easy. When we choose to believe in something (or someone), we *ourselves* take the risk of obeying the truth we have discovered. That is why I am not surprised that there is a time lag for people to be able to believe in Jesus Christ. Like the first son in Jesus' parable, the decision-making process can sometime take us well into the afternoon. These dynamic verbs of faith are each in their own way the words of struggle because God has refused to intimidate our senses and compel our obedience to his will. Sometimes it takes time to believe. The trying out of options and examination of evidences must somehow come together so that we are able to trust in the trustworthiness of the promises of God.

There are times when I have thought I wanted to pray that the Holy Spirit would so dramatically impress the truth of God's love and faithfulness upon a particular person that he or she could not help but believe. But this is a prayer that ignores the very gift of dignity and responsibility that God has already impressed upon each human being (see Gen. 1-3; Matt. 7). The Holy Spirit confirms and assures, but the Holy Spirit does not cancel out our freedom to repent and to discover and to believe. Our Lord's parable of the prodigal son (Luke 15) insists upon this freedom, as do the gospel narratives of Christ's many encounters with various individuals (for example, the rich young ruler in Mark 10).

Very often people will unthinkingly seek the overwhelming of the senses for themselves or for others, but what they may really want is a seduction experience, an experience of being overwhelmed by God's majesty so that their choices are pushed aside by the glory of the experience of an awesome God. They may pray fervently for such a spiritual breakthrough but inevitably they are disappointed by the noncompliance of the one who knows what we need better than we do. He answers a deeper question than we asked, but his answer takes more time than we expected.

There are exiting and awesome human experiences of the presence of God, and we are fortunate to experience the wonder of such crisis moments of worship. However, they are meant to lead us toward a larger journey, just as the disciples' mountain-top experience of seeing Jesus being transfigured before their very eyes was not something that could be enshrined (Matt. 17:1-6). In *The Silver Chair*, we hear the words of C.S. Lewis words about grief: "Crying is all right in a way as long as it lasts. But you have to stop sooner or later and then you have to decide what to do."[1] The same principle is true of the subjective "hearing" experiences of faith. An awesome experience is all right in a way as long as it lasts. But it will stop sooner or later and then you have to decide what to do.

THE TRUTH WILL MAKE YOU FREE

The mystery of faith is that the Holy Spirit confirms and assures a human being who is en route in the journey of deciding whether to trust God or not. That Holy Spirit assurance preserves both the freedom of God and the freedom of the human being who is deciding to believe. Now we can understand why, in the New Testament teaching concerning the Holy Spirit, the promises of freedom are present in the same context as the promises of assurance. For example in John 8 our Lord tells his disciples, "You will know the truth, and the truth will make you free . . . . If the Son makes you free, you will be free indeed" (John 8:32,36).

We experience freedom on our way into faith and once we own faith as our own decision we experience even more freedom! This is the mystery: How is it that God is able to keep his own freedom—remember our Lord's words to Nicodemus: "The wind blows where it wills" (John 3:8) and, at the same moment, be able to preserve in our individual journeys our real freedom, "For freedom Christ has set us free" (Gal. 5:1)? When we look closely at the language of faith we are better able to understand how this is possible because the words are inescapably words of our own choice, just as they are of God's grace.

We are the ones who hear; no one can do it for us or make us do it. Jesus fully recognizes this freedom ingredient in the word *shama* by his decisive use of the phrase, "He who has ears to hear, let him hear." We can make the same observations of every other faith verb because each one is a word that we must decide about. We must repent; no one can do it for us. Our Lord put it this way in his great parable of the prodigal son, "But when he came to himself he said . . . 'I will arise and go to my father'" (Luke 15:17-18). We must praise God with our own words and acts of praise, and however amateurish or inept our worship expression seems to us, nevertheless it is just that form of praise which honors and pleases God.

Perhaps now we can see that, on the whole of it, the most dangerous thing of all could be any religious training program that is designed to make the ordinary Christian less ordinary and more expert in the methods of faith.

Paul's call to each of us is to "present our bodies in view of the gracious kindness of God" (Rom. 12:1). This call is still the best call, and it invites each of us as ordinary people to present our real selves to Jesus Christ because he is good—totally and permanently. Therefore, he will know what to do with us when we dare to trust in him. This act of the faith that responds to the evidence of God's character is the act of the non-expert who decides, perhaps into the afternoon, to trust in the faithfulness of God. Such an act may involve a lot of struggle, but very little training in religious practices or ceremony is needed.

QUESTIONS FOR FURTHER STUDY

1. What kind of thoughts and feelings do you have toward the word *hear*?

2. What does the word and the way it is used in Deuteronomy 6 tell you about faith?

3. When someone says to you, "I hear you," what do you think
   that person is saying?

4

FAITH IS A
GOOD NEWS WORD

1 Thessalonians 1:1-9

When we have faith it means that we have trusted in a message of the good news after testing its truthfulness. What does this mean? Faith's object is the very character of God; its subjective enactment happens as a real human being discovers that trustworthiness of Jesus Christ so that I decide to trust in God. But in the journey of trusting, in the thousand single steps of faith, it is the message about God's self-disclosure that makes sense to me so that I decide to trust in the center of that good message, the living person Jesus Christ.

This brings us to a third set of words in the faith vocabulary of the Bible. These are the *good news* words, the words of assurance and argument. Probably the most interesting of these words is the Greek word *pleroma*—this New Testament word is translated by the English words "convince" and "fulfill."

What happens in the journey of faith is that the witness to Jesus Christ, which we call "the good news" or "the gospel," becomes reasonable, and as I listen to its arguments, I am convinced of the truthfulness of the message itself. But more than that, there is a further discovery that is required for faith to happen. I must discover the relevance of the message about God's mighty acts and self-disclosure to the real world and the life I now am living. Christ may be true in some encyclopedic sense but the real question is: What difference does he make? What difference do his promises make if I were to trust in them?

Each human being is fine-tuned in such a way that the puzzle pieces that need to come together in order to fulfill this set of questions and longings varies from person to person. The things each of us needs to know in order to be convinced of the relevance and the truthfulness of the gospel are unique to each one of us.

Because the consciousness of each individual's search for meaning and life fulfillment is different, each person looks at evidence from a different angle and needs awareness. Jeremiah wants to know *why*; Job wants to know *who*; David wants the resolution of profound inner conflicts and sins; Peter needs assurance of his own worthiness after his failure to remain loyal to Jesus on Good Friday. The list is a long one, especially when each of us logs in his or her own felt needs.

Good news, to be really good, must meet us where we are— where we hurt, where we are straining at the boundary and where we are broken and unable to find the energy to strain any longer. Therefore, for the issue of faith to become understandable to real people in real places, there must be a vital connection made between the promises of God and the people who hear those promises. We are fortunate because the good event from which the gospel owes its very origin has this inherent personal and interpersonal relevance. Nevertheless, we must always ask that question and test the answers we find.

THE GOSPEL IS CONVINCING

When we read the New Testament closely we notice that most of the documents that come together to form the gospels and the letters were written in order to explain and make sense of the gospel so that we who read the documents would be convinced intellectually, morally, and internally. Luke tells his friend Theophilus why he writes the gospel and sends it to him: "So that you may know the truth concerning the things of which you have been informed" (Luke 1:4).

This is also the note in what was probably the first book of the New Testament, Paul's letter to the Thessalonians: "For our gospel came to you not only in word, but also in power and in the Holy Spirit and with full conviction" (1 Thess. 1:5). "Full conviction"—here is that word *pleroma* again. The Christians of Thessalonica, a district capital of Macedonia, had been convinced of the reality of Jesus Christ to such an extent that Paul reminds them that they "turned to God from idols, to serve a living and true God" (1 Thess. 1:9). To put it another way, the message that Paul shared with the people made sense to them and won their respect. It made more sense to them than the wide selection of Greek and Roman myths. There cannot be faith without this sense of confirmation.

There needs to be the good news that wins our respect. In order for this to happen, God must himself take a great risk. He will speak in the law and the prophets and permit the human family to react to the speech. But even more, he will speak by the ultimate humiliation of total identification with the human

43

family in that one who, in the words of G. K. Chesterton, is the "enormous exception" of all time, Jesus Christ our Saviour-Lord.

The gospel tells the story of that long journey of self-disclosure, and we decide to trust in God because we have thought through the gospel and its message has won us. We see from this the imperative significance and importance of the Bible as a book for us in our quest and our journey of faith. This is because it is the Jesus Christ of history in whom we believe. It is because of the events of the life, death and victory of Jesus of Nazareth that we have decided to trust.

When I think back on my own journey I remember the importance of the small Bible study group I attended at Barrington Hall while I was a sophomore at the University of California in Berkeley. That group Bible study put the New Testament into my hands so that I was reading through young adult eyes the witness to the man Jesus of Nazareth. What happened was that the character of that man won my respect. In the beginning days I did not read the Bible as the word of God. I read it the same way I would read any other book. But what happened was that the Old Testament by anticipation and the New Testament in witness pointed me toward its living, personal center—Jesus Christ. The Lord at the center won my mind's attention, and this was followed by another milestone, as the hero of the text won my respect and then my heart.

The mysterious part for me happened when I was able to put my weight down upon the trustworthiness of Jesus, and an assurance dawned upon the whole of me that the love of Jesus is "also for me."[1] More than a general truth, this good news was now *my* truth. The love I met in the biblical witness had pointed me to events that took place among real people in real places. I had discovered that love is not a theory or altruism or benevolent kindness in the abstract, but rather that love is the event by which God acted toward us within our actual historical story. This mixture of words of promise and events of grace is the reason why we can know that in fact we are also loved twenty centuries later.

THE GOSPEL IS TRUSTWORTHY

The mystery of faith is that the Holy Spirit bears witness with our spirits so that we are able to trust in the good news and believe that we are indeed beloved by God (Rom. 8:16). In all of the New Testament's teaching on the Holy Spirit, we are assured in and through the content of the gospel message about Jesus Christ and not apart from that message. The Holy Spirit does not work against the thoughtfulness and meaning of the good news. This is why the Holy Spirit does not confirm our hearts apart from our minds. The Holy Spirit, Jesus tells us, is the Spirit of truth (John 14).

How different are the "spirit" experiences in Greek mythology! In Greek mythology the influence of the gods toward human beings is both overwhelming and irrational; people are swept off their feet and their minds are clouded, their choices are canceled out. Not so in the experiences of the people of the New Testament. "The Holy Spirit," writes John Calvin, "is the bond by which Christ binds us to himself." When we are bound to Christ our minds are clearer than ever before to ask all of the tough questions; our freedom is more decisively active than when we thought we were the masters of our own kingdoms.

When we believe in Jesus Christ our respect for all truth and the mandate upon us to search for truth in every field of human exploration is heightened. This is because there is a built-in alliance between the Lord of Truth and every truth. This alliance has the practical effect of encouraging in the believer the scientific spirit of enquiry and basic everyday curiosity. Reason is therefore sharpened—not dulled—by a growing Christian confidence in the trustworthiness of God. There is a reality orientation at the heart of Christian faith because it is the God of truth whom we believe in, and in whom we are to grow as believers. For this reason, I always advise Christian students to pursue the windy landscapes of academic studies and scientific research with the realization that they have been granted in Christ an exciting mandate to discover truth in each corridor of the great house we call the created order.

Blaise Pascal, the famous French mathematician, was as right as he was clever when he made three observations about humanity:

> There are only three sorts of people: those who have found God and serve him; those who are busy seeking him and have not found him; those who live without either seeking or finding him. The first are reasonable and happy, the last are foolish and unhappy, those in the middle are unhappy and reasonable.[2]

Yes. *Reasonable* is the word for it. In the grand search of the human mind and spirit, our reason is at work. In authentic Christian faith our reason stays fully alert and alive.

QUESTIONS FOR FURTHER STUDY

1. What are your reactions to the following sentence? "The gospel of Jesus Christ must win our respect before we can believe."

2. Does Paul in his opening paragraph in the letter to the Thessalonians give us clues as to why the people in that city believed in the gospel?

3. What do the words "living and true" in 1 Thessalonians 1:9 mean to you? How do you define them for today's setting?

5

DYNAMICS OF FAITH

Galatians 2:11-21; Acts 14:25-15:11

One of the most electrifying encounters in the New Testament takes place between Paul and Peter at Antioch. This confrontation is vitally important for the young Church of the first century because it led to the settling of a central question about Christian belief.

Paul has preserved for us that encounter by his retelling of the incident in the letter to the Galatians:

> But when Cephas [Peter] came to Antioch I opposed him to his face, because he stood condemned. For before certain men came from James, he ate with the Gentiles; but when they came he drew back and separated himself, fearing the circumcision party. And with the rest of the Jews acted insincerely, so that even Barnabas was carried away by their insincerity. But when I saw that they were not straightforward about the truth of the gospel, I said to Cephas before them all, "If you, though a Jew, live like a Gentile and not like a Jew, how can you compel the Gentiles to live like Jews?" We ourselves who are Jews by birth and not Gentile sinners, yet who know that a man is not

justified by works of the law but through faith in Jesus Christ, even we have believed in Christ Jesus, in order to be justified by faith in Christ, and not by works of the law, because by works of the law shall no one be justified. But if, in our endeavor to be justified in Christ, we ourselves were found to be sinners, is Christ then an agent of sin? Certainly not! But if I build up again that which I tore down, then I prove myself a transgressor. For I through the law died to the law that I might live to God. I have been crucified with Christ; It is no longer I who live, but Christ who lives in me; and the life I now live in the flesh I live by faith in the Son of God, who loved me and gave himself for me. I do not nullify the grace of God; for if justification were through the law, then Christ died for no purpose. (Galatians 2:11-21)

Paul puts it as clearly as possible: *"We . . . know that a man is not justified by works of the law but through faith in Jesus Christ . . . I live by faith in the Son of God, who loved me."* The noun/verb "faith," and all it means, is the second most significant word in that decisive encounter. Of first importance is the name Jesus Christ. Paul has put his weight down upon Jesus Christ; he trusts in God's fulfillment of the law in Jesus Christ so that he describes his faith as faith in Christ. The Greek preposition *eis* actually is even stronger—"into" is the sense of the word. Faith *into* Christ.

He tells of how both he and Peter "have believed" because of the strong choice they made. "The life I now live in the flesh I live by faith in the Son of God." Paul preserves our own freedom in choosing.

Faith is also an experience in which Paul was convinced by the evidence that he found. He challenges the Galatian Christians who have been drawn into legalism to think through the evidence for themselves: "Does he who supplies the Spirit to you and works miracles among you do so by the works of the law, or by hearing with faith?" (Gal. 3:5).

But notice what faith is not:

Faith Is Not a Leap into the Void

Faith is not a desperate act of the will that trusts without evidence. The faith that emerges in this Galatian text and throughout the Bible is a human response to the evidence we have received of the true and trustworthy character of God. God's self-disclosure of his character, his love, his faithfulness is therefore prior to our faith. Human faith trusts in that self-disclosure.

Faith is a brave rejection of the idols, but it is more than that; it is a response to the living and true God (1 Thess. 1:9). Faith is a thinking response to the living truth we discover in the Gospels.

Faith Is an Art Form

Faith is not a ritual to be mastered by those who have special skills at believing. The Galatian fascination with the legalistic—the circumcision question—has become for them a temptation to their faith. This book to the Galatians, therefore, becomes a helpful case study of this danger.

Circumcision is a Jewish faith ritual in which a family by faith would lay claim upon the ancient promises made by God to Abraham. The ritual is a sign for Jews of their identity connection to Abraham and to the wonderful promises made by God to Abraham.

Paul is not prepared to discard this ritual as a meaningful sign in Israel. However, he will not allow the sign to become more than a sign. The reality is greater than the sign, and the reality is that Jesus Christ has fulfilled the promises made to Abraham so that now, "There is neither Jew nor Greek, there is neither slave nor free, there is neither male nor female; for you are all one in Christ Jesus. And if you are Christ's, then you are Abraham's offspring, heirs according to promise" (vv. 28-29). This means that we are invited to bring ourselves to God just the way we are, slave or free, male or female, Greek or Jew.

We are heirs of Abraham by faith; therefore, we do not need to perform any of the signs of identity that have a fixed place in Jewish tradition, but because of their fulfillment in Christ they as signs are now of secondary importance to what is of fundamental importance; and that is our relationship with Jesus Christ. The implications of this clarification by Paul are far-reaching. It means that the focus of attention is not upon the methods of faith or acts of faith but upon the object of faith. Therefore we should not become preoccupied with the fulfillment rituals of believing.

When a preoccupation with spiritual technique or methods of the legalistic kind does take place we find ourselves caught up in the entrapment into which both gnosticism and legalism eventually tumble. The irony of the legalistic redefinition of faith is that "faith" simply becomes a new name for an old pattern of "works." Our salvation is falsely seen as dependant on the rites of faith more than it is upon the Lord of faith.

But Christian trust in God means that I bring my real self to the Lord. It is "problematic me" that belongs to the event called "faith" as I bring myself to God with all of the complexity that makes me who and what I am. It is this real self that comes to Christ in response to his truth, his love, his reality. The evidence of who Christ is draws me to trust the goodness of Christ with the complex mixture of who I am.

This real self, "problematic me," is the person I bring to the Lord when I am a believer (Rom. 12:1-2). I trust my real self to Christ and I show by this act how much confidence I really have in God. God is not surprised by my weaknesses (see Rom. 8:26) and, therefore, it is important to preserve this amateur nature of the act of believing.

A student once said to me, "I'll be able to believe in the Lord as soon as I can resolve a few problems."

We talked for a while about the problems and they were significant ones, and I said to the student: "On the basis of what you know about the character of Jesus Christ do you think that he cares about these problems that are really bothering you?"

The student said that he felt his answer would be a qualified yes. It was more like, "Yes, I hope so."

Then I made one last suggestion: "Why not bring the negative problems as well as your positive conclusions to this Jesus Christ of the New Testament at the same time. You have real problems that are confusing and complicated but you have great respect for the Jesus Christ of the New Testament. Why not collect the two threads together and bring them both to Christ."

Here is faith; it is just this real and definite and just this tentative too. The student, who stood in front of me, needed to make the best move he could honestly make toward the Lord Jesus Christ. He needed to know more about Christ, but he already knew enough to make a first move (tentative though it was) when he wagered on his statement, "Yes, I hope so." He will discover how solid indeed is the love of Jesus Christ, but right now he needs to move on the basis of what he now knows. The Reverend Sam Shoemaker of Pittsburgh once put it this way: "Faith means giving as much of myself as I know to as much of Christ as I know."

FAITH IS NOT ABSOLUTE

The third important result comes from Paul's defense of faith. Paul realistically invites the Christians in Rome who receive his letter to bring their incomplete and even fragile faith directly to God so that the Holy Spirit will resolve for them what is lacking in their faith journey. He puts it this way:

> Likewise the Spirit helps us in our weakness; for we do not know how to pray as we ought, but that very Spirit intercedes with sighs too deep for words. And God, who searches the heart, knows what is the mind of the Spirit, because the Spirit intercedes for the saints according to the will of God. (Romans 8:26-27)

What we learn from this is that faith is not absolute. Only God is absolute. Our faith trusts in God, but since it is our faith that does the trusting it cannot be absolute. The mystery of the Holy Spirit's confirmation and assurance of our experience of believing means that faith is a gift from God. Nevertheless, the mystery of the gift is this assurance of the Holy Spirit that does not destroy our real freedom. This freedom preserves the relative and non-absolute nature of faith as a genuinely human experience. Because of this we can correctly describe our faith as an experience both of growth at certain times in our journey and of decline at other times in our journey. Some people grow in faith and some people see their faith fade. This dynamic nature of faith is then both its glory and its crisis.

God is so sure of himself that he allows us to have this freedom of experience with all of its joyous surges and its dry valleys, its doubts and its affirmations, its determination to trust when evidence seems to vanish. Our faith can be tempted and it can also be encouraged because our faith is a freedom journey. We never have absolute proof because there is no such thing. The decision of God to preserve our real humanity makes such intimidation of our senses an impossibility for his design.

C. S. Lewis illustrates this point as clearly as I've seen it through the comment of his senior devil, Screwtape, in *Screwtape Letters*.

Screwtape cannot understand why God, who Screwtape calls the "enemy," does not make more use of his almighty power. He comments to Wormwood:

> You must have often wondered why the Enemy does not make more use of his power . . . But you now see that the Irresistible and Indisputable are the two weapons which the very nature of his scheme forbids him to use . . . He cannot 'tempt' to virtue as we do to vice.[1]

We do not have the proof that sweeps away every question. We might expect that from Zeus but not from the God and Father of our Lord Jesus Christ. What we have instead is just enough evidence to assure us of the love, the integrity, and the faithfulness of Jesus Christ.

I remember a young man who came in to talk with me when I was Minister to Students at University Presbyterian Church in Seattle. He was struggling with serious doubts that he had about the existence of God. I asked him what he needed to know. He told me what he needed was an absolute proof of God's existence. I then asked him to name such a proof and I would try my best to respond once I knew the proof he needed. He then looked out the window of my office at the church and pointed out a tree on the church property. "If I could see that tree split in two by lightning at exactly 12:05 p.m. today that would be an absolute proof and I'm sure it would help me out a lot."

I suggested that before we make such a request could we imagine that in fact the request had been honored and it was now 12:06 p.m. with the tree perfectly split by lightning. I then asked him the big question. "What has this miracle proved?" As we talked for awhile we both agreed that the tree-splitting event certainly has not proved the existence of God, but only the existence of some spiritual power only slightly above our physical realm of existence which is willing to amuse the human beings on NE 47th Street.

There is also the possibility of coincidence, which cannot be completely ruled out. It could have been an accident or coincidence. But the philosophical fact is that the sign does not "prove" what this student asked to have proved—even though he himself set up the criteria for the proof. But what is even more important is that the sign on NE 47th Street did not prove what we both wanted most to know. The sign told us nothing about the character of God, his love or his trustworthiness.

Here lies the dilemma for all those who demand absolute reasons and "absolute" assurances from God. These "absolute" proofs are impossible because, as Pascal points out, "we do not trust our senses" and, therefore, each day we would need a more dramatic proof to prop up a faith misplaced in the first place.

God is absolute, and that is why there are no absolute proofs for us, because both we and our faith are not absolute. We trust in the evidence that God knows we really need to know, and that is the evidence of grace and truth. We do not have all the evidence, but when we have enough and when we have eyes to see and ears to hear, then we believe in God.

QUESTIONS FOR FURTHER STUDY

1. In what ways do think of faith as an "experience" or a "journey"?

2. What is the experience that took place at Antioch? Describe the parts and how each part fit in with the next part?

3. What were the dangers or temptations to faith in Christ that emerged at Antioch?

4. Give your own definition of Christian faith on the basis of Galatians 2 and Acts 15.

6

THREE REASONS FOR FAITH

Galatians 2:11-12; Acts 14:25-15:11

Trusting in the evidence of the truth and the love of God is a journey more than it is a single act. When I trust in the character of God, that trust is an event, but it is a moving, non-static event. We trust on the basis of evidence.

Pascal put it this way:

> There are three ways to believe: reason, tradition [habit], inspiration. . . . We must open our minds to proofs, confirm ourselves in it through habit, while offering ourselves through humiliations to inspirations, which alone can produce the real and salutary effect. *Ne evacuetur crux Christi.*

Ne evacuetur crux Christi—"No escaping the cross of Christ." The mystery of what Jesus Christ has done on our behalf must be the final proof and that confirmation belongs to God alone. The evidence comes from God himself who assures us of himself in different ways: through history, through the reasonable tests of the implications of believing and through inspiration. This means we begin with the events in history of the life and ministry and teaching of Jesus Christ. But the mystery of what Jesus Christ has done in our behalf must be the final proof and that confirmation belongs to God alone.

ASSURANCE THROUGH HISTORY

The narratives about the life of Christ are the opening four books of the New Testament, the four Gospels: Matthew, Mark, Luke and John. But the history that substantiates our faith in Jesus Christ goes back behind the New Testament into the sacred Scriptures we call the Old Testament. They anticipate the radical intervention in history of our Lord and they play their own vital part in the journey toward faith. The Law, the Prophets, the Psalms and the historical narratives of the Jewish people in the history of their nation—these are a decisive part of the evidence of God's self-evidence. Through the grand design of the Law, the poetry of Israel's longings, the stern judgement as well as the hope and promises of the prophets, all mixed together with the sometimes disturbing narratives of Old Testament history we are brought to the one who stands as the fulfillment of every people's journey—Jesus of Nazareth.

This means that both the goodness and the awkward tragedies of Old Testament history bring us in their own way to this fulfillment. When we have finished reading the Old Testament we like the psalmists yearn for the Messiah who will be able to do two things: (1) to fulfill the greatness of the Law's design, and (2) to resolve the tragic incompleteness of the Law's people. The fact that people who were contemporary to Jesus trusted in his fulfillment of these two yearnings is an encouragement to our faith. The fact that men and women through the continuing journey of history have trusted in Jesus Christ is also an encouragement closer to our own time and circumstance.

This assurance from tradition has a very practical importance for me in my own autobiography of believing. The faith of St. Augustine and St. Paul has had real influence upon me and my faith, as has Pascal's faith and the stormy faith of Martin Luther and Dietrich Bonhoeffer. I am encouraged by those I have known personally who believed in Jesus Christ: Dallas and Mary Birch, Dick Jacobson, John Blaul, Colt Maxwell and Jean McMillian.

This is what Pascal is telling us: Our trust in God is commended to us by the church as it is spread out across the windswept markings of human history. In an ironic way, both in courage and in defeat, the stories of the believers are an encouragement to our faith. The Messiah must be able not only to fulfill King David's awesome greatness but also to resolve David's raw sinfulness. The very real sinfulness of the church, both in the New Testament and in the centuries since, draws us to the Redeemer through *crises*. The courageous faithfulness of the church and the Christian heroes of faith draw us to the only Redeemer in another way—because of *greatness*.

ASSURANCE THROUGH REASONABLE TESTS

Faith is reasonable; and one of the ways we become believers in Jesus Christ is that, when we put his Lordship to the test and experiment with the implications of faith in Christ, we are convinced by the fact that faith that trusts in the character of Jesus Christ makes sense; and it works in real life here and now.

I have often encouraged people who are trying to discover the reality or unreality of the gospel to test the evidence by an examination of the results and possible implications of believing in Christ. Since we are able to think through alternatives and options in the rest of our decision-making processes, why not do the same in the whole question of the credibility of faith in Jesus Christ? We need to try out the implications of faith.

If I were to believe in Jesus Christ and trust in his love and faithfulness, what effect would that trusting have in my life? Would I look at the world differently? How would I understand myself in the perspective of his self-disclosure to me in the gospel? How would I look at the people around me? What ethical implications would emerge from faith in Christ, and would those ethical results be positive or negative? Since it is the Jesus Christ of history that I am asked to trust, what effect would my confidence in that historical Jesus and his promises have upon my intellectual stance toward the world? Were I to trust in this Jesus Christ that I discover through the biblical witness, then how would I relate my life to the biblical documents that surround him and now gain their own authority in borrowed fashion from that living center? Would the doctrines and meanings that I would build from the Bible benefit from this biblical authority as source or am I better off making up my own doctrines independently? These are the kinds of experimental questions that reason must pose in order to test that "All authority in heaven and on earth has been given to me" (Matt. 28:18).

C. S. Lewis has developed his argument in favor of Jesus Christ precisely in this experimental way. He puts it unforgettably by means of a parable:

> Let us suppose we possess parts of a novel or a symphony. Someone now brings us a newly discovered piece of manuscript and says, "This is the missing part of the work. This is the chapter on which the whole plot of the novel really turned. This is the main theme of the symphony." Our business would be to see whether the new passage, if admitted to the central place

which the discoverer claimed for it, did actually illuminate all the parts we had already seen and "pull them together." . . . Something like this we must do with the doctrine of the Incarnation.[2]

Lewis' point is that when Jesus Christ is the center he draws together the parts that cannot otherwise be integrated into a meaningful whole. They come together with such a surprise that even the hitherto neglected details now make sense too.

ASSURANCE THROUGH INSPIRATION

Finally, the main evidence of faith is the evidence of God's self-evidence, and it must be the decisive influence if we are to believe; this what Pascal means by the word "inspiration." It is God himself who must assure us of Jesus Christ by a way that preserves both his own freedom and our freedom as well. We may speak of faith as a "gift," in this sense, provided we know what we are really saying.

Faith is a gift but it is also our own journey, just as marriage becomes a gift when a young couple allows the priest or pastor to present to them their wedding rings which they then place upon each other's hands in the name of the Father and the Son and the Holy Spirit. But marriage is also a decision made by two people because we are free to leave home and make a new home, because we are free to commit our lives and our futures to each other in the present and toward the future. This freedom is a freedom *from* the past, a freedom *in* the present and a freedom *toward* the future. At the same moment it is also true that marriage is a holy estate, and as such it is a gift to be received from the Lord.

We become believers because of three kinds of evidence. Our experience with each of the evidences may be emotionally stormy or quite a logical assessment of data; but somehow the parts—like parts of a great life puzzle—come together and make sense so that we decide to trust the weight of our lives upon the faithfulness of God's self-disclosure, Jesus Christ.

QUESTIONS FOR FURTHER STUDY

1. Pascal tells of three reasons for faith: tradition, reason, and inspiration. Do you sense one or more of these reasons in Luke's brief letter to his friend Theophilus at the opening of his Gospel?

2. What happens to be Luke's concern as he writes to his friend? From this greeting, what do you expect to find in this book?

3. What do you think John means by use of the words "signs" in his statement at the close of his book?

7

FAITH AND WORKS

James 2:18; Galatians 3:4-5

"But some will say, 'You have faith and I have works. Show me your faith apart from your works, and I by my works will show you my faith" (Jas. 2:18). These words of James, when they have been rightly understood, have encouraged the church. But their misreading has also confused the church at times. The confusion has to do with what James means by the word *works*.

The Greek word *erg* (translated here as "works") is the same word the Apostle Paul uses in 1 Thessalonians 1:3, and which he in the same way as James connects to the word *faith*. Paul is thankful to God that the Thessalonians are experiencing "your work of faith and labor of love and steadfastness of hope." *Erg* means work as an event; whereas the word *kopos* "labor of love" means work as hard and sweaty toil. Therefore, what both Paul and James mean by their uses of this word *erg* is that faith is an event that concretely happens, and when it works itself out in acts of love it also has its hard work aspect too.

When the Apostle Paul contends against salvation by "works" in Galatians 3:4, what he is contending against is not the concreteness of faith, but against the idea that I and my works are my own gospel. The gospel is not that I work hard to please God or even that I work hard at having faith. Our act of believing is not the gospel any more than is the good news the good works which we manage to do. The gospel is possible because of God's mighty act of saving love in our behalf at the cross. The gospel is, therefore, the surprising news that this grace is for us and that we may now trust the Lord of that grace and enter into a living relationship with Jesus Christ.

THE DANGER OF BAD DOCTRINE

The bad doctrine of salvation by works is a real danger that always lurks at the edges of our freedom theology. We have vital decisions to make in response to God's acts toward us; our faith; therefore, and our experience of repentance is our decision and no one else's. No one can repent for us; but that does not mean that our acts of repentance thereby become our salvation.

Repentance and trust, just as love and hope, are responses on our part to the act of God on our behalf. This is the great truth that Paul is seeking to keep clearly focused for the Galatian Christians who, in their case, are in danger of overrating the importance of the ancient covenant signs of identity, especially circumcision. Paul had no argument against Greek men who desired to identify with Israel's history of promise by accepting the sign of circumcision. But when he saw that this sign was granted more importance than it deserved, and when he saw that Greek Christians were trusting in that sign to assure them of their relationship with God, then the Apostle Paul forced the crisis that required the assembly of the first ecumenical council of the church at Jerusalem (see Acts 15). At that council the issue was settled that God's act in Jesus Christ alone stands at the center, and our relationship to God in Jesus Christ is by faith alone. It is this confidence alone that makes a Christian and enables a person to stay a Christian. Notice how St. Luke records this event in the history of the church:

> But some men came down from Judea and were teaching the brethren, "Unless you are circumcised according to the custom of Moses, you cannot be saved." And when Paul and Barnabas had no small dissension and debate with them, Paul and Barnabas and some of the others were appointed to go up to Jerusalem to the apostles and the elders about this question...
>
> The apostles and the elders were gathered together to consider this matter. And after there had been much debate, Peter rose and said to them, "Brethren, you know that in the early days God made choice among you, that by my mouth the Gentiles should hear the word of the gospel and believe. And God who knows the heart bore witness to them, giving them the Holy Spirit just as he did to us; and he made no distinction between us and them, but cleansed their hearts by faith. Now therefore why do you make trial of God by putting a yoke upon the neck of the disciples which neither our fathers nor we have been able to bear? But we believe that we shall be saved through the grace of the Lord Jesus, just as they will" (Acts 15:1-2. 6-11).

Each new generation in the church must face this crisis of sign "inflation," and we must always insist upon the truth that we are not ourselves the gospel. We are tempted by our own fascination with each new advocacy in the church to embrace some particular old or new sign of obedience or spiritual breakthrough and then to judge our Christian neighbors by how they relate to our new inner discovery. But the gospel is *extra nos* (outside ourselves) before it becomes *intra nos* (inside ourselves). Just as we are able to love in the Christian sense because God first loved us, so we speak our faith because God first spoke his faithfulness.

God calls us to act, and our faith is a dynamic response on our part to that call. This means that our faith itself is not the gospel but it is a freedom event.

THE DANGER OF A NEW BONDAGE

Paul warns us in his freedom letter, Galatians, of the danger of a new bondage and loss of freedom that arises from our desire to have signs of covenant. This desire for signs may shift the essential center of our confidence away from Jesus Christ himself toward some other motivational and integrative center. When such a shift has happened we have lost our freedom in Christ and have entered into bondage.

As I see it, this "Galatian problem" has had many duplications through the centuries since Paul first wrote his letter. The "isms" that have grown up at the edges of the Christian Church have often drifted toward a replacement of grace as God's all-sufficient speech for himself in Jesus Christ toward some other "new" advocacy or urgency which is meant to prove our real sincerity as Christians.

Each proposed "new" emphasis, or ancient truth now uncovered, becomes a new center—a false one. This is Paul's concern in his attack upon anything that might separate us from God's will for our lives. The new concern, which now is the new center point, may claim that it is very old, as in the case of legalistic fascination with some aspect of the *Law*. The new concern may be very avant-garde, as in the Gnostic claims to exciting spiritual breakthroughs. But in each instance there is at first a subtle shift away from the all-sufficiency of Jesus Christ and, finally, a dismissal in actual practice of his central importance as the new movement has completed the entrapment of its followers.

C. S. Lewis puts the strategy of this shift into the mouth of his senior devil, Screwtape, as he gives advice to the tempter, Wormwood, with regard to a "patient" that Wormwood is trying to win away from Christ:

> My dear Wormwood, the real trouble about the set your patient is living in is that it is *merely* Christian. They all have individual interests, of course, but the bond remains mere Christianity. What we want, if men become Christians at all is to keep them in the state of mind I call "Christianity And". You know—Christianity and the Crisis, Christianity and the New Psychology, Christianity and the New Order, Christianity and Faith Healing, Christianity and Psychical Research, Christianity and Vegetarianism, Christianity and Spelling Reform. If they must be Christians, let them at least be Christians with a difference. Substitute for the faith itself some Fashion with a Christian colouring.[1]

Lewis's last line is just the point: the best way to lure a Christian out of authentic faith is to find a "substitute for the faith itself." This is the great concern of Paul. There is no theme advocacy, no tradition new or old, that deserves to be at the center apart from the mere Christianity of our confidence in Jesus Christ himself.

THE FREEDOM OF A LIVING RELATIONSHIP

Therefore, for both Paul and James, it is the event faith that grows out of the gospel that sets us free. We need no other gospel but the gospel as it powerfully works its way throughout the many corridors of our daily lives. Our greatest freedom comes from the living and growing relationship we have with the Lord of the good news, Jesus Christ. When we are bound to

Jesus Christ and his lordship we are in the profoundest sense free to be all that we were meant to be.

The Pacific Northwest is windy, especially at the water's edge, where the land meets the cold waters of the Puget Sound. The small town of Mukilteo is particularly windy and therefore the perfect place to fly a kite. There are always on non-rainy weekends a large group of children and adults, with string in hand and kites in the wind. The very concept of kites is a fascinating study in incongruity: The fragile combination of ultra-thin paper fastened to small pieces of wood, the colorful tail of rags and the inevitable string that attaches the kite to its flyer on the ground.

I have wondered about the parable that is hidden in the flying of kites. Let us suppose that a kite could think for itself. It might say these things to itself: *Here I am high in the wind of the Saratoga passage and I feel the powerful lift of the wind, but I also feel an equally strong pull toward the ground from this string attached to my center and held tightly by that small child. The whole arrangement is wrong. If it weren't for that string with which I am held back I could really fly. I know it because I feel the power of the wind trying to push me higher, but the flyer on the ground is holding me down. I'll secretly bring a pair of scissors on the next flight and then watch me soar!*

The rest of the story of this parable is no surprise to flyers of kites. The string is cut, there are sudden jolts and then the tailspin fall to the earth. Something which the kite in my parable did not know is the aerodynamic fact that it was the very tension of the connection of string and kite and the flyer on the earth that made the kite's flight a possibility in the first place. It seemed logical for the kite, on the basis of the feelings of wind pressure and the downward tug, to conclude that the youngster on the ground was hindering it. But these feelings were not a true or accurate readout of the total situation. The kite needed the ground flyer even though the string put the kite itself under strain. The strain was a good strain. The tension a good tension. This is a parable that shows the sometimes stressful but nevertheless healthy relationship between freedom and truth.

In the spring of 1993, at the University Presbyterian Church in Seattle, I shared this kite parable as a part of a sermon I gave on the theology of the Holy Spirit. I was illustrating John Calvin's comment: "The whole of it comes to this, the Holy Spirit is the bond by which Christ binds us to himself." I made the point that in the Bible we receive our greatest stride and fullest freedom when we are bound to the truth. "You will know the truth, and the truth will make you free" (John 8:32). I told the kite parable to illustrate that reality. The next week a friend of mine, Bruce Bailey dropped by the church and told me that during my sermon on Sunday he had jotted down a poem that came to him as I told the parable. He had written it on a three-by five-inch card and he assured me I was free to quote it if I thought it would be appropriate. The next Sunday I quoted the poem, "I am the Kite":

I am the kite;
Red and orange,
Fire in the sky,
Stunt kite,
Cutting loops
And gashes in the blue,
Skin vibrating
On frame bent with power.
I cut the cord

To fly yet higher still,
To show the rest
What freedom's all about.

I turn and twist
My fanciest curl
And set a course
For distance.
But my mistake
Was not
To take the wind for granted,
But the cord
That tensioned me
To one I did not see
So far below.
The flyer is not me.

The congregation loved the poem, and we published it the following Sunday. I actually quoted the poem for several Sundays because its theme was so much in tune with my series of expositions on the theology of the Holy Spirit.

Some three weeks later I was handed an anonymous poem (though the writer later identified herself to me as the writer). This poem, entitled "The Kite Tangled in the Tree," also proved to be very powerful:

The other kites are flying free
But I am tangled in a tree.
My heart is crying with despair,
Will I ever be up there?
Torn and tattered how can I be
Ever up there flying free?
The string is tangled in more than one limb.
The future for me seems so dim.
God has been healing, but it takes so long,
And the gale-wind forces seems so strong.
What will happen to a kite like me
Tangled, so tangled, in a tall, tall tree?
Will I ever be
Up there with the other kites flying free?
Able to trust the breeze and the string,
Able to trust God in everything?

A month later I received another poem—"I am the Balloon"—
from a writer who had sent me several poems before. I still do
not know who he is, though one of his other poems tells me that
he is a man in his thirties or forties. He wrote a note with his
poem in which he told me that his poem started as a spoof on
the original kite poem. "But," he wrote, "something happened to
me midway through the poem":

I am the balloon:
Blue and green,
Flying in the sky.
Stunt balloon?
I laugh at the kite below
"cutting loops and gashes in the blue."
(I grow weary of hearing his poem.)
his power is not his own.
I have no cord to cut.
My power comes from within.
Talk about convergence?
I soar miles above Mount Shasta
As the kite flutters helplessly
To the trees below.
I ascend into the stratosphere
Growing large and more powerful
As I rise.
But whoa! What's this!
I'm feeling tight!
What was that sound?
Oh my. I fear I'm just a wad
Of latex on the ground.
Here comes that kite-flyer.
I hope he doesn't step on me.
His hands are warm.
He is stretching me on a cross!
I am a kite!!
Amen

It is a fact about human life that we function best and are freest to reach our greatest human potential when we trust truth, and keep connected to truth, and when we experience the tender hands of the one who is the Truth. Our connection to Christ will often create intense strain upon us, but the strain is basic to living, and it is the strain that creates growth.

To break the connection to what is true produces a false kind of freedom—it is like the 1,500-meter runner who decides to take his final sprint across the grass midfield to the finish line. Such a runner only appears to come in first, but his victory is not founded in reality. It is like a "marathon" runner who joins the race halfway through the race. We thrive most when we keep our connection to righteousness, even though that connection may curtail certain kinds of freedom, such as sneaking across the field in the 1,500-meter race.

Righteousness holds us accountable like the string on the kite, but it is the accountability that makes the flight possible. In the same way our accountability to God's will works in our favor. We discover our real adequacy when God's truth is the tie that binds us, but our frailty is matched by the surprising power of God's grace.

QUESTIONS FOR FURTHER STUDY

1. In what way is faith a concrete event?

2. Do you feel a strain upon your Christian faith by James' words in James 2:18? What is the strain?

3. Do you feel a strain upon your Christian faith by Paul's words in Galatians 3:4-5?

4. Can you write a definition of faith that includes both Paul's Galatian concern and James' concern?

8

BUT SOME DOUBTED

Jeremiah 12:1-20; Matthew 28:16-20

Now the eleven disciples went to Galilee, to the mountain to which Jesus had directed them. And when they saw him they worshiped him; but some doubted. And Jesus came and said to them, "All authority in heaven and on earth has been given to me. Go therefore and make disciples of all nations, baptizing them in the name of the Father and of the Son and of the Holy Spirit, teaching them to observe all that I have commanded you; and lo, I am with you always, to the close of the age." (Matthew 28:16-20)

It is not easy to believe when the world has come undone. The disciples who met Jesus in this dramatic incident, recorded by Matthew, trusted in Jesus Christ so much that they obeyed him and worshiped him. This means that, on the basis of the evidence they had experienced, they were willing to trust in Jesus. They did not have all the evidence, but they had enough. Nevertheless, alongside all of this and even after the Easter victory of Christ, the Gospel writer Matthew tells us that some of the disciples still doubted! They trusted, but there were some questions about which they were still unsure. Matthew is realistically candid with his readers in pointing out the fact of this uncertainty.

JEREMIAH'S FAITH

There is a kinship of this Matthew narrative and the turbulent faith of two Old Testament heroes: Job and Jeremiah. They trusted God, and yet at many hard moments during their journeys they were still discouraged enough to express their doubts. Listen to Jeremiah in his complaint to the Lord:

Righteous art thou, O Lord,
when I complain to thee;
yet I would plead my case before thee.
Why does the way of the wicked prosper?
Why do all who are treacherous thrive?
Thou plantest them, and they take root;
they grow and bring forth fruit;
thou art near in their mouth
and far from their heart.
But thou, O Lord, knowest me;
thou seest me, and triest my mind toward thee.
Pull them out like sheep for the slaughter,
and set them apart for the day of slaughter.
How long will the land mourn,
and the grass of every field wither?
For the wickedness of those who dwell in it
the beasts and the birds are swept away,
because men said, "He will not see our latter end."
(Jeremiah 12:1-4)

Now listen to the Lord's reply to his prophet Jeremiah:

"If you have raced with men on foot,
and they have wearied you,
how will you compete with horses?

And if in a safe land you fall down,
how will you do in the jungle of the Jordan? (Jer. 12:5).

We listen to an honest Jeremiah with his stern complaints about the wicked people in his city, but Jeremiah the prophet hears hard words himself.

Matthew's portrayal of faith in the concluding chapter of his Gospel, though not as stormy a portrayal as that of Jeremiah, still shows that faith in God is a realistic and complicated decision which men and women make against real odds. Matthew shows us that we make that decision in the very face of unanswered questions and struggles of the soul.

We are now able to understand how free and freeing God's grace toward us really is. God must be very sure of himself—if he were not, he could never permit our doubts to accompany our faith in the time lag between our hearing his call and doing his will. Job, like Jeremiah, decides to believe despite his own doubts, the accusing judgments of his advisors—even the crushing despair of his wife. His faith wagers on hope, but that faith cannot ignore the intense and haunting pressures of the doubts.

JOB'S FAITH

There are complicated possibilities present in the faith-decisions of Job: When my son Jon was in college, he wrote a paper[1] on Job for a course on Western civilization. It is well worth quoting here:

> The Book of Job shows a character who, despite pain, loss, and suffering, cleaves to and trusts God, his afflictor. Concurrently, Job keeps his integrity by asking questions and making demands as a result of his unwarranted pain. To cling to God in faith is unreasonable from the secular viewpoint. Similarly,

Job is unreasonable from the religious, God-fearing viewpoint to make demands in the face of God's justice and omnipotence.

What do we do with the doubts and the demands like those of Job and Jeremiah? Or those of John the Baptist? Deitrich Bonhoeffer? Martha? Peter? What about our own doubts and the crises of faith that each of us must face during the act of deciding whether or not to trust in the faithfulness and love of God? Job's wife in the crisis of her own personal and family devastation had decided to permanently reject any possibility of the goodness of God; therefore, her counsel to Job is brutally clear in its total disappointment. She tells Job to "curse God and die" (Job 2:9).

> Job's wife can no longer understand his loyalty to God and presents the secular alternative to praising him by saying, "Do you still hold fast your integrity, curse God and die" . . . For her, the reasonable choice and natural instinct when someone or something inflicts pain is to move away from or curse it.[2]

The other advisors of Job are friends who observe his crisis; they have themselves a stance that is apparently more protected and less vulnerable than that of Job or his family. But their advice is equally devastating. My son has this to say of them:

> Four characters Eliphaz, Bildad, Zophar, and Elihu . . . must be considered the voice of religion, which says that Job shouldn't question God, he should question himself.[3]

Job himself chooses the hardest of all responses:

> Job faces and demands to deal with God, the root of his problems: "But I would speak to the Almighty, and I desire to argue my case with God" (Job 13:3). He also draws hope from his choice to love and trust God. "For I know that my Redeemer lives . . ." (Job 19:25) . . . No solution to suffering exists, but resignation doesn't even deal with the problems.[4]

Job has chosen a hard road, but it is the right road. He decides to bring his doubts to the Lord just as he had earlier brought his praise and adoration to the Lord. In the surprise ending of Job, God tells Job's advisors, "You should have listened to Job."

It is the mystery and wonder of faith that this very act of sheer honesty and directness becomes a very rich part of what the Bible means by believing in God.

It is still true that the experience of doubt is not a pleasant experience. There is an unsettledness and loneliness about all doubt, whether it is the doubt of God, of neighbor or of ourselves. Therefore, we must now more closely examine the nature of our doubts so that we are better able to understand ourselves as well as our Christian faith.

FAITH IS BOTH A NOUN AND A VERB

Faith, in the vocabulary of the Bible, is both a noun and a verb. This means that we are the ones who believe, which is the verbal nature of faith. We believe in God's faithfulness, which is the noun of faith. Since we know that God has such awesome authority within himself it is not unreasonable to expect that God should use his power more forcibly to reduce the very possibility of doubt on the part of we who are human and limited. This expectation seems at first glance to be a logical result of the grand dimensions of the nature of the noun, the object of our believing.

But when we journey through the biblical narratives with the men and women who believed in God, and when we watch the ways in which they grew in their faith, we are confronted with the story of the remarkable restraint and self confidence of God. The God of Abraham, of Job, of Martha and of Paul is not the manipulative Zeus. He does not override the human will or "cancel us out." Our integrity and our freedom are preserved throughout the narratives of biblical faith, and it is precisely this preservation of our journeying experience that makes the possibility of doubt an inescapable part of the whole story for many disciples on the way. To our surprise, doubt can even become a healthy part of our spiritual journey.

THE DOUBT CYCLE

The dynamics of doubt are as complex as are the dynamics of faith, and it is important that we try to make sense out of the doubt cycle that operates in every normal human relationship in the same way as we must understand the faith cycle. The phenomenon of the late afternoon downward stress in the biological rhythm of the human body has its parallel in the human personality (see diagram below).

There is the *honeymoon period* for most relationships with people and ideas—not just for newly marrieds. This is followed by a solid, somewhat slower *period of settling in* and settling down.

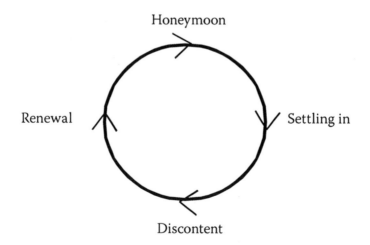

Honeymoon

Renewal

Settling in

Discontent

But as disappointments and frustrations begin to add up, this building period moves inevitably toward another part of the arc in the relationship journey that might be called a *period of disillusionment or discontent.* The disillusionment may be of a vague and generalized form or it may have very precise stress points of injury and disappointed expectations.

It seems to me that at just this part of the arc in the cycle an individual is confronted with a strong desire to break away from the arc itself and move on to a new and uncomplicated arc of fresh discovery and honeymoon satisfaction. It is a fact that, in an urbanized and individually isolated society, it is possible to easily disconnect from relationships that seem entrapped in that downward slope of the arc. The options of divorce, interpersonal mobility, employment mobility or convictional mobility then often present themselves to us as the swift solution for a long afternoon disillusionment experience.

It appears on the surface that the strategy of disconnection works as a solution to disillusionment. But what has really happened is that a whole new community of isolated and incomplete human beings are tempted to live out their lives in a blur of self-pity and expectation letdown. These half-circle persons fail to make the best discovery of life, which is the full-circle discovery of *renewal* (forgiveness, resolution) and then the joy of relationships that have made it around the total circle from romance to grace, from honeymoon love to fulfillment love, from youthful faith to seasoned faith.

There are others who resist or are too frightened for some reason to attempt even the strategy of breakaway during the arc of disillusionment, and they decide to stay stale and make compromised bargains with cynicism and defeatism. There are people who need a catastrophe to stir up the afternoon's depression so that renewal can happen. It is never too late, but for some it is very late before the staleness and experience of burnout is interrupted by grace.

Highly affluent and mobile cultures are occupied by many folk who have rarely stayed in a relationship all the way around to full acceptance and the joy of grace. The sojourners of disappointment have established a pattern of leaving the church when it lets them down, dropping their friends when the demands of real friendship are tiring, walking away from Bible study when the assignment is tough, leaving the room when an argument needs to be talked through. It is a quiet though devastating pattern, and when it is allowed to take over our lives unchecked it becomes a gradually impenetrable armor plating against the best of all gifts and the richest friendships. It produces the permanent low-grade doubter who may gradually empty the self of all vulnerability and feeling.

Doubt is something we are to use against and alongside the foundation stones to test them, but it is not itself a foundation upon which a house may be built. This is its limitation. Therefore doubts need to be resolved so that their honest questions may take their good and healthy place in the arc of the circle but do not destroy the circle. Every relationship needs to go the full circle and we should not be unduly frightened by any part of that circle as long as it stays a part of the whole circle's journey.

QUESTIONS FOR FURTHER STUDY

1. Is there a difference between complaint and doubt? How do the words relate to each other?

2. Why might some of the eleven disciples still be in doubt as recorded in the final paragraph of Matthew? Can you think of reasons for this doubt?

3. Are you surprised by the answer that Jeremiah hears from the Lord or that the disciples hear from Christ?

4. Do you feel those answers prepare the way for the resolution of doubt?

9

FOUR KINDS OF DOUBT

John 1:43-51

"That man's doubts are like the doubts of a horse, neither of them has thought about the matter," wrote Samuel Johnson. It is important to study our doubts just as it is important to study our beliefs, and when we do make such an investigation, the first discovery we make is that there are different kinds of doubt and different kinds of doubters.

DOUBT AS A PRIMARY REFLEX

I have a friend who always seems to say about every subject, "I don't know about that." He is a steady sort of mildly negative man who doubts as a primary reflex. His doubt is like that of Samuel Johnson's doubting horse.

Puddleglum is one of the best and most interesting characters in the *Chronicles of Narnia*, and he is just the sort of doubter who proves that reflex skeptics can be very good people. Puddleglum doesn't think anything will turn out right, and he doubts very much whether anything will work the way it is supposed to. But, nevertheless, with a little urging from his two young English friends he does come through. In the end, Puddleglum and his doubts have a big part to play in saving everyone's life.

He is obstinate and basically suspicious of everything for a little while. That "little while" turned out to be good because it led to the rescue of the Prince as well as of Jill and Eustace who had fallen under the spell of the Emerald Queen in the underneath world. Puddleglum was not as impressed by the Queen as were the other pilgrims, and when he put his foot in the fire the terrible smell of burnt marsh-wiggle cleared everyone else's head too. The character of Puddleglum illustrates that reflex doubt is not altogether harmful, though such people need the enthusiasm and encouragement of strong believers around them at all times.

DOUBT AS AN INSTRUMENT OF LEARNING

There are other people who make skillful use of doubt as an inquisitive instrument of learning. They doubt in order to learn and to clarify. Nathanael is just this kind of doubter (see John 1:46). He skeptically raises the kind of questions that do not become roadblocks to discovery but, in fact, help to sharpen the focus of what is really taking place. "Can anything good come out of Nazareth?" he asks. This is a very good question, quite apart from its expressing possible disdain for a mountain village. Philip does the right thing when he meets up with the skepticism of Nathaniel—he invites him to experience the reality himself: "Come and see for yourself, Nathanael."

THE PESSIMISM OF PERMANENT DOUBT

There is one form of doubt, however, that is altogether dangerous to the human personality. It is the *skepticism that becomes permanently protective.* It is the faithless fog that, like ether, keeps a man or woman who is accustomed to inhaling it protected from the possibility of grace but not from the possibilities of despair. Such doubt produces its own energy of sadness and critique which often becomes a brilliantly painful pursuit of the permanent crisis of meaning for the human journey. Some of the greatest poems, novels and literary works of our own century have had their origin in this doubt of everything, a skepticism painful and earnest. Doubt itself does no permanent damage to the soul so long as a search is still taking place. But when it settles and becomes comfortable as a cynicism of closed-off expectations, such doubt is the sickness unto death. We who observe one another are never really certain where the dividing line is, but wherever it is cynicism it is a grave danger to the soul. It is the horror that Kurtz in Joseph Conrad's *Heart of Darkness* finally recognized at the end of his life, but too late to make any difference in the way he lived his life.

Much of the twentieth-century existentialism has embraced this kind of doubt and such stories as *Endgame* and *No Exit* have explored the unreasonableness of life that is the direct result of permanent doubt. T. S. Eliot's *The Hollow Men, The Waste Land*, and *Prufrock* do the same. But the pessimism of permanent doubt will finally lead toward either escapism or radical resolution.

The escapism of drugs and pornography have their own philosophical origin in just this hopelessness of permanent doubt. If the evening is etherized why not the patient too? (T. S. Eliot, *Prufrock*). It is a fact that sexual pornography, which is a form of violence against women and men, has its origins in the permanent doubts we have about ourselves and our genuine worth. Pornography is a deadly escapism that so completely doubts meaning that it decides to watch non-meaning in an endless repetition of confusion and interpersonal exploitation.

Radical resolution is what happened to T.S. Eliot when, in spite of himself and his doubts, he discovered the love of God. Many other pessimistic doubters have made the same discovery. That discovery haunts every other pessimist as well. Jean Paul Sartre, the twentieth century's most entrenched literary atheist, was to write in his final published book *Words*, "I only trust those who only trust God and I do not believe in God; try and sort that out." It makes us wonder about the final completeness of his doubt and the certainty of his pessimism. Even one of my favorite filmmakers, Woody Allen, the self-affirmed permanent cynic, is whimsically but earnestly searching for the meanings of redemption in his 1984 film *Broadway Danny Rose.*

HUMOROUS DOUBT

There is still another kind of doubt which I like best of all. It is the *humorous doubt* that is born of grace. I am describing the doubt of intentions and pretensions that has grown up out of the sheer realism of knowing myself and my own need for forgiveness. This self-knowledge that comes from grace makes such a person more realistic and less gullible to his or her own pretensions as well as the claims and promises of others and the causes they affirm.

Every church, every family, and every nation needs such doubters. This kind of doubter is decidedly not pessimistic, nor is he or she foolishly optimistic. They have been mellowed by the experience of the gospel of Jesus Christ in which their own real sin is honestly faced and resolved day in and day out; and because of that experience they can never forget their own present need for forgiveness and need for growth in grace. This biblical realism makes them doubters of the grand claims of every idealism and also of the grave doomsday announcements of hopeless pessimism. Such a person is a doubter of each announcement because the gospel has cleared his or her head.

ESSENTIAL DOUBT

Deciding major questions is not a simple matter, especially when help is being offered. Imagine the following scene: A solo 185-pound mountaineer is at the final stages of his climb of a steep mountain peak and he has carefully pushed his gear over the final edge of the summit. But just at this moment he temporarily loses his footing and begins to slide perilously toward a sheer drop-off. Just in time he is able to grasp hold of an exposed root near the edge. He cannot better his footing without help but at least he is temporarily safe—not for long but at least for a while.

The climber shouts for help and waits hopefully. At this moment, our story is complicated as someone shows up at the edge of the cliff and reaches over, putting his hands around the climber's arms and offering to help him get better footing. The problem for the climber, however, is that he must let go of the root for the few seconds it takes to get better positioned with new footing. But if he lets go of the root where he is now safe, even if only temporarily, and trusts himself completely to the grip of his helper, he for those seconds might find himself in greater danger than before, because for a few seconds he is completely in the hands of his rescuer.

The question is: What will determine whether or not the climber lets go of the root? I know of two all important determining variables: (1) it depends on what the climber thinks of the goodwill of the helper, and (2) it depends on what he thinks of the strength of the helper. The one variable has to do with the moral question of the intention and integrity of the helper, and the second variable has to do with the substantial question of the durability and authority of the helper.

Let us suppose the climber looks up and the one he sees offering help is an old enemy from school days. He recognizes the person as the anti-mountaineer who may have been the one rolling rocks down upon him during his climb. Will he let go? No! Because he does not trust the goodwill of the one who offers help. He would rather take his chances with the root

Think of a second possibility. A cub scout troop is on a nature hike at the summit and one of the smallest boys in the pack has heard the climber's shouts. This small boy is now the one who places his small but sincere hands around the wrists of the climber. Will the climber let go? No! Not for the same reason as before, because even though this lad has total goodwill and wants very much to help, the problem is one of substance. The climber knows his own weight and knows that his new friend's offer of help is sincere but inadequate. Were he to let go of the root then both of them would tumble toward the sheer drop-off.

The one case is an instance of the climber's distrust of the goodwill of the supposed helper; in the second instance, the climber distrusts the authority of the supposed helper. He cannot risk at the place where he now is safe, though the safety is temporary, unless the two variables are answered positively in his mind. Otherwise, his faith would be foolishly entrusted.

I see this imaginary story as a psycho-drama that puts in focus two great questions concerning our faith in God's promise of help that is found in the gospel of Jesus Christ: (1) Can we trust the promises of God as they are fulfilled in Jesus Christ, the one who offers ultimate help to us? (2) Is Jesus Christ able to keep the promises he has made? The one question wonders about his love and the second wonders about his faithfulness; the one about goodwill, the other about substance.

QUESTIONS FOR FURTHER STUDY

1. If Nathanael is a doubter, what kind of doubter is he? How would you describe his doubts?

2. In what ways is doubt useful to faith?

3. How would you explain the difference between helpful doubt and destructive doubt?

10

THE DOUBTS OF DISAPPOINTMENT

Luke 7:11-35

Doubt has many forms and many subtle complexities. Doubts about God that I have encountered fall mainly within three groupings: First, those doubts which might be called the doubts of disappointment—*moral doubt*; second, the doubts of reason —*intellectual doubt*; third, the doubts of the self—*internal doubt*. Each of these kinds of doubt is found in the biblical narratives and throughout history whenever people in whatever century have decided to trust in God. Doubts are not irresolvable, but neither are they easy to solve.

MORAL DOUBT

One of the problems for modern novelists, as I see it, is that the characters in their stories are so often superficial and humorless. Because of these "thin" people, we who read their adventures in the twentieth-century novels and plays do not suffer with them when they supposedly suffer, and we do not laugh as much as we should when they supposedly laugh. Thinness is the problem.

Even as talented a writer as John Updike cannot make his readers feel anything but casual curiosity as the lives of each married and unmarried couple fall apart and away in his novel *Couples*. No one matters that much in the story and they all seem to get what they deserve. As Updike himself would put it, their stories are like the paint that doesn't stick to anything. They are vague and shallow people who drown in vague and shallow water. I have wondered if Updike, being such a brilliant writer, actually intended his readers to come to this very conclusion.

It is curious that the best drama and the best novels of our century have solved the literary problem posed by such characters by concentrating upon the superficiality itself as the essence of tragedy. Willy Loman in *Death of a Salesman* by Arthur Miller is just such a character. His wife must plead with her son to "pay attention" to Willy. Why is it so hard to pay attention to the salesman? This question becomes the tragic question in the study of such a hollow man who nevertheless is a suffering man.

There are a few exceptions. Films such as *Chariots of Fire*, *Good Morning Vietnam* and *Gandhi* portray characters who are by nature substantial in themselves. But the exceptions prove the basic rule that since it is difficult to find great virtue in life it becomes equally difficult to portray great tragedy in life.

John the Baptist was a person who would tower over his counterparts in any generation. He was born and reared in the city, but he became the powerful prophet of the wilderness of Jordan. John dared to challenge the duplicity and corruption of his own generation wherever he saw it. He was a first-century Stormcrow who like Gandalf, the wizard in *The Lord of the Rings*, stalked both the powerful and the weak with the word of judgment, the call of repentance, and the promise of hope.

He won followers who stayed loyal to him long after his death (see Acts 19) and, as a popular folk hero, John the Baptist was more famous in Palestine than was Jesus of Nazareth. He was the people's prophet, the one who prepared the way for the coming Messiah. His words were salty and uncomplicated:

> He said therefore to the multitudes that came out to be baptized by him, "You brood of vipers! Who warned you to flee from the wrath to come? Bear fruits that befit repentance, and do not begin to say to yourselves, 'We have Abraham as our father'; for I tell you, God is able from these stones to raise up children to Abraham. Even now the axe is laid to the root of the trees; every tree therefore that does not bear good fruit is cut down and thrown into the fire."
>
> And the multitudes asked him, "What then shall we do?" And he answered them, "He who has two coats, let him share with him who has none; and he who has food, let him do likewise." Tax collectors also came to be baptized, and said to him, "Teacher, what shall we do?" And he said to them, "Collect no more than is appointed you." Soldiers also asked him, "And we, what shall we do?" And he said to them, "Rob no one by violence or by false accusation, and be content with your wages."
>
> As the people were in expectation, and all men questioned in their hearts concerning John, whether perhaps he were the Christ, John answered them all, "I baptize you with water; but he who is mightier than I is coming, the thong of whose sandals I am not worthy to untie; he will baptize you with the Holy Spirit and with fire. His winnowing fork is in his hand, to clear his threshing floor, and to gather the wheat into his granary, but the chaff he will burn with unquenchable fire."
>
> So, with many other exhortations, he preached good news to the people. But Herod the tetrarch, who had been reproved by him for Herodias, his brother's wife, and for all the evil things that Herod had done, added this to them all, that he shut up John in prison. (Luke 3:7-20)

John the Baptist was the one who first announced Jesus as Lord, and he did it in a way that sought to transfer his own popularity in the eyes of the masses toward the Messiah. Each Gospel records John's comment about Jesus as one "whose sandal I am not worthy to untie" (John 1:27, see also Matt 3:11; Mark 1:7; Luke 3:16). Something of the esteem of the crowds towards John is indicated by the fact that he is even able to make such a comparison. It is only in the recognition of the greatness of John the Baptist that this analogy of his makes any sense.

Then came a series of disappointments for John. They began early! The Lord's first meeting with John was a disappointment to the great prophet and Matthew records that first encounter in a way that points up the disappointment.

> Then Jesus came from Galilee to the Jordan to John, to be baptized by him. John would have prevented him, saying, "I need to be baptized by you, and do you come to me?" But Jesus answered him, "Let it be so now; for thus it is fitting for us to fulfill all righteousness." Then he consented. (Matthew 3:13-15)

John's baptism, in his own mind and by his clear explanation to the people, was a baptism of repentance and preparation for the Mighty One who was now to baptize with fire and with the Holy Spirit. John had not expected the apparent neglect and avoidance by Jesus of that expectation. Nevertheless, Matthew makes it clear that Jesus came to the Jordan and insisted upon his own way with his prophet.

It is possible that John was also confused or disappointed that Jesus departed from the places of Jordan or the urban hills of Judah for rural Galilee. It is in Galilee where Jesus carried out the largest part of his ministry. Why would Jesus stay away from the center of greatest religious and political influence?

One catalyst that would have intensified the discouragement of John even more was his own imprisonment stemming from the corruption and conspiratorial intrigues of the house of King Herod. This second rate protagonist, Herod Antipas, whom Jesus had called the "fox" (Luke 13:32) lived from 4 B.C. to A.D. 39. He was not respected by his own countrymen, and his reputation was further damaged when he married the wife of his brother Philip. John had challenged Herod, and for that challenge the great prophet would lose his own life. Luke makes a spare but implicative comment, "But Herod the tetrarch, who had been reproved by [John the Baptist] for Herodias, his brother's wife, and for all the evil things that Herod had done, added this to them all, that he shut up John in prison" (Luke 3:19-20).

There is an especially harsh kind of brutality in the entrapment and humiliation which John experiences. He deserves better than this. But in it all his friends stay loyal to him, and through them he is able to reach out toward the one he had called Messiah. He sends his friends to find Jesus in Galilee and through them he asks the biggest question of his life: "And John, calling to him two of his disciples, sent them to the Lord, saying, 'Are you he who is to come, or shall we look for another?' "(Luke 7:19).

This is moral doubt; the doubt of a man who is profoundly disappointed in the moral and spiritual leadership of Jesus Christ. John had expected that the messiah would eradicate evil. Its many poses and swaggering arrogance would be destroyed like the chaff that is thrown into the fire. Instead of this long-awaited prophetic fulfillment, he heard the reports of the ministry of Jesus in Galilee; he was told of the Lord's acts of healing and of the raising of a widow's son in Nain (see Luke 7:11-17). But John is disappointed perhaps because he had clearly expected more religiously and politically important things to happen. He had hoped that Jesus would engage the forces of evil on a bigger stage than in the small towns of the north.

John's doubts are very significant because he had believed so much. The downfall of Zhivago in Pasternak's great novel, *Dr. Zhivago* is so much more shattering than the downfall of Freddie in Updike's novel *Couples.* The reason is that, in the first instance, Zhivago is a substantial and weighty man, whereas Freddie is lukewarm and trivial. We cannot take Zhivago lightly as we do Freddie, and though we disagree with a particular course of action he may choose, nevertheless we suffer with him when he suffers. His doubts and his failures are more profoundly felt because his beliefs and his greatness were so real.

I feel the same deep sense of grief when I read the simple words of Luke as he tells of the doubts of the great man John the Baptist, the one whom Jesus had called the greatest man (see Luke 7:28). These are doubts that shake the world because they come from a man who had once been so certain of the world's foundation cornerstone. John calls into question the most central affirmation of his life with this skeptical question of his: "Are you the one who was to come, or should we expect someone else?" (see Luke 7:19).

THE INTENSIFICATION OF DOUBT

John is not the only figure in the Bible who has encountered and experienced the doubt of disappointment. We see this doubt in the troubled questions of Jeremiah (see Jer. 12) and of those who murmured against Jesus because of his willingness to eat and accept the hospitality of tax collectors and sinners (see Luke 15 and 19). The Pharisees were disappointed by what they saw as the disregard and carelessness of Jesus toward the observance of the fourth commandment regarding the Sabbath.

In each of these examples we meet up with the doubt of disappointment, and the story is still not finished. Great and small questions unsolved still cause men and women to doubt the goodness of Jesus Christ or the moral objectives and goals of Jesus Christ. Sometimes the objections are very small; nevertheless, the doubt may have the same result.

I remember hearing Becky Manley Pippert tell the story of a student fellowship gathering to which she had been invited. After the meeting she had a conversation with a student who had sought advice because she felt troubled. Becky invited the student to share some of the doubts that were causing her such distress. The student recounted the deep experience of doubt she was feeling because she had, on several occasions, requested the Lord's help for a problem she was facing; she had felt no help from the Lord even though she had prayed sincerely.

Becky was trying to be sensitive to this crisis of faith and asked if it would help if the student shared the problem with her. At this point the student said she had a terrible problem with letter-writing and that she had asked repeatedly for spiritual help with this problem, but to no avail, and she was weeks behind in correspondence. Becky pondered her friend's crisis and realized that what this young woman really needed was a greater crisis.

Often the approach of our Lord to the doubts of disappointment is to stir up an even greater crisis for the doubter. This is also what happens to Jeremiah when he contends with the Lord. The Lord's reply is a good example of crisis intensification: "If you have raced with men on foot, and they have wearied you, how will you compete with horses?" (Jer. 12:5). In other words, "The crisis is going to become even more intolerable for you, Jeremiah."

Jesus frequently took the same approach toward those who were troubled by his acts of healing on the Sabbath, thereby breaking Sabbath law in their view of it. In John 5, he tells the crowd, after he has healed the man at the Bethesda pool, "My Father is working still, and I am working" (John 5:17). This statement did not answer their doubts about his obedience of the Sabbath law, but, instead, it moved the doubt to an even deeper level. The questioners must now face the greater question of Jesus' identification of himself with God the Father.

But the doubts of John the Baptist require no intensification because he has done that for himself by the question he decides to ask of Jesus, "Are you the Messiah or shall we look for another?" What John has done with the various reasons for his disappointment is to draw each reason and unanswered question toward one total and all-encompassing question. It is this question he brings to Jesus in the best way he can.

RESOLVING GREAT MORAL DOUBTS

How are such great moral doubts as those that confronted John the Baptist resolved?

Ask Deep Questions

The beginning of the resolution is initiated in the question John decided to ask. He had himself done what Jesus also did toward those who were disappointed with his generous healing friendship toward sinners and his apparent abuse of the Sabbath law. Our Lord elevated the questions to their greatest intensity and their most radical possibility. In the same way, John did not decide to ask questions about Jesus' ministry timetable or about his places of ministry—instead he asks the most basic question: "Are you really the Messiah?"

This is the radicalization of the question—whether it is done by Jesus himself or by his questioners. Those angry about the offense of the Sabbath had even more to be angry about when Jesus finished speaking at the Pool of Bethesda. "This was why the Jews sought all the more to kill him, because he not only broke the Sabbath but also called God his Father making himself equal with God" (John 5:18).

There can be no resolution of the deepest questions until we try to ask the deepest questions. Therefore, the courage to ask the hardest question is the first step toward the discovery of faith from within the crisis of moral doubt. John the Baptist takes that way as his own.

Call Out to God's Faithfulness

The second step is that John the Baptist decided to bring his question to Jesus. He turned toward the Lord with his disappointment. The personal pronouns are important. He did not ask abstractly, "I wonder if *he* is the Messiah?" Rather, he turned toward Jesus form his prison cell and sent his disciples to ask, "Are *you* the Messiah?"

We are now standing at a crossroads in which doubt and faith unite into one catastrophic convergence point where it is possible to say that, at this precise moment, John the Baptist became the man of greatest doubt and the man of greatest faith. His doubts were overwhelming but he brought his doubts to Jesus; he turned to Jesus for his answer. This turn toward Jesus is what faith is at its profoundest level.

We are strongly reminded of the "roar" of Psalm 22:1: "My God, my God, why hast thou forsaken me?" This is the cry of moral doubt, and it is also the cry of faith that is shaken but which, nevertheless, calls out to God's faithfulness, personally and directly.

Jesus' reply to John as recorded for us by Luke is both profoundly understated and generous. Jesus honors his friend and speaks to him with dignity and with mystery. Jesus quotes Isaiah 40 and 61 to his friend and assures the world's greatest prophet that he, John, had not run his race in vain (Luke 7:21-27):

> In that hour he cured many of diseases and plagues and evil spirits, and on many that were blind he bestowed sight. And he answered them, "Go and tell John what you have seen and heard: the blind receive their sight, the lame walk, lepers are cleansed, and the deaf hear, the dead are raised up, the poor have good news preached to them. And blessed is he who takes no offense at me."
>
> When the messengers to John had gone he began to speak to the crowds concerning John: "What did you go out into the wilderness to behold? A reed shaken by the wind? What then did you go out to see? A man clothed in soft raiment? Behold, those who are gorgeously appareled and live in luxury are in kings' courts. What then did you go out to see? A prophet? Yes, I tell you, and more than a prophet. This is he of whom it is written,
>
> > 'Behold, I send my messenger
> > Before thy face,
> > Who shall prepare the way before thee."

The words and the deeds of Jesus mixed together were the resolution for John the Baptist as they have been for many doubters since John's lonely and honest act of faith.

In Matthew's narrative of this same event, after our Lord completed his statements concerning John and the ministry of the great prophet, he turned toward the people and said, "Come to me, all who labor and are heavy laden and I will give you rest" (Matt. 11:28).

Remember Jill who, in the novel *The Silver Chair*, is sobbing uncontrollably after a great crisis event? C. S. Lewis (the storyteller) makes this observation: "Crying is all right in a way as long as it lasts. But you have to stop sooner or later and then you still have to decide what to do."

The same can be said of the doubts of disappointment.

"Doubting is all right in a way as long as it lasts, but you have to stop sooner or later and then you will still have to decide what to do."

QUESTIONS FOR FURTHER STUDY

1. Describe some disappointments you know of or have personally experienced that challenge your faith?

2. How do you relate them to the doubt experiences of John the Baptist?

3. How does Jesus respond to John the man and to John's doubts?

11

THE DOUBTS OF REASON

John 20:24-29

When we trust in God it involves our head as much as our heart. Faith is a response to the evidence, but what happens when we have serious questions about the evidence? These are doubts of reason—*intellectual doubts.*

The first creed of Christian faith consisted of three words, *Jesus Christ Lord*; and the earliest affirmation of that great fact by the New Testament church consisted of their preaching about the life of Jesus Christ, his death on our behalf, and the triumph of Easter. Peter's first sermon makes the cross and the resurrection of Christ the foundation stone of his sermon: "But God raised him up, having loosed the pangs of death, because it was not possible for him to be held by it" (Acts 2:24).

Paul fully agrees with Peter, and in the opening sentence of his letter to the Romans he affirms the same great truth that "Jesus Christ our Lord" was attested "Son of God in power according to the Spirit of holiness by his resurrection from the dead" (Rom.

1:4). But we know from both Luke's and John's Gospels that it was not an easy matter for the disciples to believe in the victory of Jesus Christ over death.

The disciples on the road to Emmaus (Luke 24) had a very hard time believing that central fact. John tells us in even more detail of the intellectual doubts of the disciple called "the Twin." The other disciples had met Jesus on Easter day, but not Thomas:

> Now Thomas, one of the twelve, called the Twin, was not with them when Jesus came. So the other disciples told him, "We have seen the Lord." But he said to them, "Unless I see in his hands the print of the nails, and place my finger in the mark of the nails, and place my hand in his side, I will not believe." (John 20:24-25)

Thomas doubts the report of the resurrection that his friends have expressed to him. It is not so much that he doubts Jesus, nor is he morally disappointed. The fact is plainly stated by Thomas that if he could be certain that Jesus of Nazareth was truly alive he would then believe in the good news that his friends, the other ten disciples, have announced to him. But he must be certain.

Thomas is not willing to risk other possibilities: Perhaps the disciples have seen an angel. This would be an impressive experience and it was the means of divine confirmation to the mother of our Lord as well as to the father of John the Baptist (see Luke 1). But Thomas demands a greater certainty than assurance of angels. He demands a confirmation of the victory over death from the one who died. There are other dangerous possibilities, too. Perhaps the disciples, as a result of fatigue and profound grief, have become victims of their own hopes or of hallucinations or even of ghostly visions. Each of these possibilities are rejected by Thomas' demand for physical evidence of the hope.

What Thomas is really saying by his demand is this: "I know Jesus, I was with him and I was his disciple during his three years of ministry and the terror-filled days of this past week. If that man is alive, then I will believe; but I will not risk my faith upon any other ground. I will not accept the comfort or assurance of angels or spiritual feelings of hope from disciples. I certainly will not risk my faith upon the strong wish that each of us has that Jesus Christ's victory *ought* to be true."

When Thomas' doubt is expressed in theological and philosophical terms it becomes the central theological question of all time. The question is this: Who is the Jesus Christ of Christian faith? This is the most fundamental question. The Jesus of history actually lived and carried on a ministry to people, told parables, healed the sick, faced judgment of a Roman governor and died upon the cross.

This Jesus was a friend of Thomas as well as the larger circle of men and women who traveled with the apostolic band. It is this man whom Thomas trusted and it is this man whom he will trust if he can be certain that it is he who lives. The Christ of faith upon whom the Church shall be built and in whose name the gospel shall be proclaimed must be, for Thomas, inseparably united to the very same Jesus of Galilee and Jesus of Holy Week. There can be no separation for Thomas. This is the theological force of his demand. For Thomas, the Jesus of history and the Christ of faith must be the same person. The question we must ask today in our century is the same. But how is such a doubt as this to be resolved?

RESOLVING INTELLECTUAL DOUBT

First, the most obvious observation is still a valuable one: *Thomas explained what he needed to know.* He put his crisis of faith into words and, in effect, established a working criteria, a means for resolution in the best way he could express it. "Unless I place my hand in his side, I will not believe."

It seems to me that this is a very good approach to take on our part toward ourselves and toward those we know who are struggling with intellectual doubt. I have often asked this very question of myself and of people who have sought out my advice concerning the reality of Christian faith: "What do you need to know?" I have asked some people to write a poem about it or a narrative stream-of-consciousness description of the question. I think the Christian fellowship would do well to listen to these statements when they are expressed and examine them closely, because the best theology always faces up to the best questions. Thomas has asked the really important question, and he found a way to say it that was definite, direct and uncomplicated.

There is a sentence in John's Gospel that gives two more vital insights into the resolution of Thomas' intellectual quest: "Eight days later, his disciples were again in the house, and Thomas was with them" (John 20:26).

My second observation is that, even though Thomas had serious intellectual doubts, *he stays with the people who have faith*. For eight days Thomas has waited with them, and he has waited without compromising his integrity. He has resisted the temptation to agree in order to please his friends; nevertheless, he has not rejected either them or their faith.

He stays in the fellowship of believers with his doubts, as hard as that is to do. It is not easy because there is an understandable uneasiness that tends to pull the doubter away from the company of believers. When the friends pray and rejoice at the assurance that they feel, he experiences a sense of weariness and dissatisfaction. Finding himself suspending judgment, he feels lonely and like an attachment to the once uncomplicated fellowship. Nevertheless, he stays.

Many times I have strongly urged the doubters I have known to stay with the family of faith—honestly, and with the various questions they struggle with still in process—but by all means stay!

So Thomas stays. But we must also note that the disciples *resist the temptation to expel from their fellowship the non-believer with his gloomy storm cloud of doubts unresolved.* We have no evidence, from John's account, of group pressure upon Thomas; just the simple statement that eight days later the band was in the room and Thomas was with them. This unaffected sentence may be one of the most compelling psychological proofs we have of the reality of the resurrection of Jesus Christ and of the disciples' certitude of that reality. The surest psychological sign of the insecurity of a movement's convictions is its tendency to purge itself of non-conformists. But the other disciples are not shaken or panicked by the presence of Thomas, because they are certain of the truth of their central affirmation.

It does not mean that Thomas is their teacher during this journey toward resolution, but he is welcome to stay in their community as the journey of resolution takes its necessary course.

The fourth stage in Thomas's journey is a surprise.

Eight days later, his disciples were again in the house, and Thomas was with them. The doors were shut, but Jesus came and stood among them, and said, "Peace be with you."

Then he said to Thomas, "Put your finger here, and see my hands; and put out your hand, and place it in my side; do not be faithless, but believing."

Thomas answered him, "My Lord and my God!" Jesus said to him, "Have you believed because you have seen me? Blessed are those who have not seen and yet believe" (John 20:26-29).

By what Jesus says and does *Jesus himself affirms his victory to Thomas*; and from the man sometimes called "doubting Thomas" we hear the greatest Christocentric confession of faith in the New Testament, "My Lord and my God!" Jesus' final words express in simple indicative and straightforwardness that many who will not see the risen Lord physically, as did the early disciples, will believe in him.

THE IMPORTANCE FOR US

There remains for us to make two major observations about this event concerning its importance for us today. First, *Thomas' doubt is our gain!* This is because we know that at least one person in the apostolic fellowship insisted that the *Christ of faith* and the *Jesus of history* must be the same person. No single issue is as crucial for twenty-first century faith as this one.

Who is the Christ we believe in? Is he the highest spiritual aspirations of radical hope for life of a first-century Church? Is he the creation of post-modernist hopes and inclinations? Or is our faith placed in the Jesus Christ who loved us concretely and won the battle over the same grave that will block the light of day for each of us?

John Updike in his remarkable poem, "Seven Stanzas at Easter," has posed the question unmistakably in the same way Thomas did that first week after the first Easter.

> Make no mistake: if He rose at all it was as his body;
> if the cells' dissolution did not reverse, the molecules reknit, the
> amino acids rekindle, the church will fall.
> It was not as the flowers, each soft spring recurrent;

it was not as his Spirit in the mouths and fuddled eyes of the
eleven apostles; it was as his flesh; ours.
The same hinged thumbs and toes, the same valved heart
that—pierced—died, withered, paused, and then
regathered out of enduring Might new strength to
enclose.
Let us not mock God with metaphor, analogy, sidestepping,
transcendence;
making of the event a parable, a sign painted in the faded
credulity of earlier ages: let us walk through the door.
The stone is rolled back, not papier-mâché, not a stone in a
story,
but the vast rock of materiality that in the slow grinding of
time will eclipse for each of us the wide light of day.
And if we will have an angel at the tomb, make it a real angel,
weighty with Max Planck's quanta, vivid with hair, opaque in
the dawn light, robed in real linen, spun on a definite loom.
Let us not seek to make it less monstrous, for our convenience,
our own sense of beauty, lest, awakened in one unthink-
able hour,
We are embarrassed by the miracle and crushed by the
remonstrance.[1]

It is our gain that Thomas' quest was resolved, because his
journey to confidence helps us to risk our own wager upon this
concrete Jesus Christ.

There is also a second implication, and that has to do with
the truth mandate of Christian faith. As Christians, *we have
received in the gospel an instinct for truth,* and this incident of
the questioning integrity of Thomas the Twin has encouraged
that instinct. Because Jesus Christ is true, we never should
cut short or intimidate the quest for truth, whether it is in the
pursuit of mathematical equations or of theological doctrine.
We have everything to gain from the truth and its vigorous
enquiry, because our Lord is the author of all truth. It means
we must take the time it takes to find the truth, and then to

follow it. Nowhere in the Old Testament or New Testament are we asked to empty our minds in order to believe. Why should we not believe with our minds as well as our hearts?

QUESTIONS FOR FURTHER STUDY

1. Do you feel that Thomas' question is a vital one? Why is it important to you?

2. What advantages do we in our century have over Thomas in answering his question? What disadvantages?

3. How do you help people you meet today who are struggling with Thomas' question?

12

THE DOUBTS OF SELF

John 21

Faith is a response to evidence so that when I discover the truth and the Lordship and the love of Jesus Christ I decide to trust in Jesus Christ. This response is not without its struggles, and within these last several chapters we have considered the stressful side of the faith journey. We have examined several kinds of doubt, two of which might be called *intellectual doubt* and *moral doubt.*

Intellectual doubt raises the truth question, but intellectual questions can be resolved because the gospel is true and it makes sense. Moral doubt is the doubt of disappointment in God, but God is good and, though he surprises our expectations, alongside of the surprises he fulfills our deepest search for justice and the true good.

But there is another kind of doubt that in some ways is the hardest of all to resolve because it seems that there is nowhere to go with it. I mean the doubt that is turned inward. It is the doubt I have of myself: the exhausting spiral of *internal doubt.*

INTERNAL DOUBT

God's existence and even his love are not in question for internal doubters because they believe these are facts and eternal truths. It is just that they cannot claim them for themselves. The causes of this internal form of doubt are very hard to track down and, in many instances, the doubt itself is masked even from our own self-understanding. But whether understood or misunderstood, it is doubt of a very serious kind and it causes harm. One way of describing internal doubt is to sketch out its harmful results: Internal doubt is a loss of confidence in our ability to trust, to love, to hope. How does this happen?

Internal doubt is sometimes caused by the failures in a person's life that become faith roadblocks for a man or woman because they are unresolved. Such doubt may be caused by fatigue—physical, emotional, spiritual—so that we lose the energy necessary to focus and concentrate. Or internal doubt may by contrast be the result of apparently too much energy—what is sometimes called the flight-fright reaction. In this panic response, there is hysterical and furious activity in a way that does not draw together and integrate the self but, instead, produces an unraveling effect. Whatever the reasons for internal doubt, the result tends toward the same direction: an inability to decide or act in healthy response to God's will for our lives. We doubt ourselves to such an extent that we find it very hard to make the incremental steps of living as a beloved one.

It may come as a surprise to most of us, but I believe that at one very difficult period in his life the Apostle Peter was just this kind of man. Peter is a remarkable man and the New Testament

Gospels narrate for us the journey of this disciple with great admiration and affection. He was our Lord's choice to be the leader among the apostles. Peter is the disciple who had been the boldest, said the most, been the closest to the teacher and had received the greatest promises.

The most dramatic positive moment for Peter occurred at Caesarea Philippi:

> Now when Jesus came into the district of Caesarea Philippi, he asked his disciples, "Who do men say that the Son of man is?" And they said, "Some say John the Baptist, others say Elijah, and others Jeremiah or one of the prophets." He said to them, "But who do you say that I am?" Simon Peter replied, "You are the Christ, the Son of the living God." And Jesus answered him, "Blessed are you, Simon Bar-Jona! For flesh and blood has not revealed this to you, but my Father who is in heaven. And I tell you, you are Peter, and on this rock I will build my church, and the powers of death shall not prevail against it. I will give you the keys of the kingdom of heaven, and whatever you bind on earth shall be bound in heaven, and whatever you loose on earth shall be loosed in heaven." Then he strictly charged the disciples to tell no one that he was the Christ. (Matthew 16:13-20)

But Peter had not been idealistically shielded by Jesus and, several days prior to the events of the Holy Week, the Lord spoke realistically to his chief disciple:

> "Simon, Simon, behold, Satan demanded to have you, that he might sift you like wheat, but I have prayed for you that your faith may not fail; and when you have turned again, strengthen your brethren." And he said to him, "Lord, I am ready to go with you to prison and to death." He said, "I tell you, Peter, the cock will not crow this day, until you three times deny that you know me." (Luke 22:31-34)

Nevertheless, in spite of the promises and the realistic preparation by Jesus, the devastating events of Holy Week were overwhelming for this disciple. A personal internal collapse took place for Peter on the Thursday and Friday of history's loneliest week. Following those shattering days, he and the other disciples experienced Jesus' concrete victory over death. The texts of the Gospel tell us that the disciples were glad when they saw the Lord.

The disciples truly believed the victory of the resurrection experiences, yet Peter is still unresolved. He appears overcome and demoralized by the powerful depression of what I have described as internal doubt. He who had made the most promises had fallen the farthest in his denial of Jesus, and now he is discouraged by the grief that followed that denial. Christ's victory is still not Peter's victory, at least in his own mind.

We owe a debt to the Apostle John for the epilogue to his Gospel, because in that final postscript chapter he enables us to understand this odd and crucial spiraling crisis of Peter's and how the Lord of his journey found him and resolved his internal doubt.

For every person who has struggled with the dull pain of internal doubt this twenty-first chapter of John's Gospel is a very helpful case study. We should watch it closely and observe what takes place in the journey of faith of Peter and his friends at a hard time in his life.

RESOLVING INNER DOUBT

What are the ways in which internal doubt is resolved? I want to make five observations from John's account.

First, there is the objective fact of *Christ's triumph through the cross and empty grave*. This is the rocklike foundation stone without which there would be no resolution of any kind of doubt. The fact is that Christ is Living Lord, regardless of how Peter felt about it. Jesus is not only *our* Lord when we honor him and praise his promises, but he is *the* Lord quite apart from our confessions of faith or our feelings about our share in that concrete and actual victory. This is the place where every resolution must begin, and its implications are far reaching. It means that many discouraged and fearful people are in fact redeemed by Christ and will stay redeemed by Christ even though they are fully convinced of their own inadequacy and worthlessness.

They are very much like John Bunyan's pitiful character Mr. Fearing, who only knew the deep bass notes of his sinfulness and unworthiness before Almighty God, and who quaked in repentance far too much because he just could not really believe how much he was beloved. He lived his journey without joy and missed out on the better songs. But God's grace is greater than his fears; therefore, the feelings he concentrated on and overrated in importance did not negate the reality of the joy but only his participation in the joy during his life. He will need to learn how to play all the strings of his guitar when he enters the celestial city; but there is nevertheless a sadness for Pilgrim and the other travelers who were compelled to live alongside such a gloomy man in that he had not learned the songs here and now. Bunyan says that Mr. Fearing was a trial to Greatheart and the other pilgrims.

We must thank God that the reality of Christ's Lordship does not depend upon our praise of Christ as Lord. God's own acknowledgement is quite enough, and this vast bedrock reality stands beneath every journey of faith.

This foundation stands beneath Peter's resolution experience; but several other things happen before Peter experiences the fruit of the facts. John's epilogue shows us the beginning of his resolution in a very earthy way:

> Simon Peter, Thomas called the Twin, Nathanael of Cana in
> Galilee, the sons of Zebedee, and two others of his disciples were
> together. Simon Peter said to them, "I am going fishing." They
> said to him, "We will go with you." They went out and got into the
> boat; but that night they caught nothing. (John 21:2-3)

John's gospel narrative tells us that *Peter's friends go with
him and stay with him* during his quest for himself, just as they
had stayed with Thomas. John wants his readers to know this,
though he narrates it in a very matter-of-fact fashion. Peter's
discouragement becomes clear from what follows in this epilogue,
but I find it very significant that in his time of lonely self-reflection
and search, Peter is not turned into a solitary man who must climb
out of his valley of humiliation by himself. There are journeys of
faith that must be taken at least in some part alone, but Peter's
denial was an offense that all his friends had also experienced
and felt and watched; therefore, this is no time for Peter to wait by
himself. These companions were his support group.

The third observation: *Peter and his friends go fishing.* This
physical work was familiar to them because they were fishermen
by trade. Therefore, the night of fishing on the Sea of Galilee
provided a corridor effect for them all. A corridor is not a place
without danger or threat, because there is no such safe haven.
But it is a place that in itself is less threatened than other places.
It is a place between places, a time between times. For Peter and
his fellow fisherman, this night on the sea became such a time
between times in which they were required to concentrate on the
work at hand.

I am a strong advocate for the conscious establishment of
corridor experiences which have this very necessary role to play
for us in that they enable us to collect our thoughts, to change
deliberately the pace of our walk and to reestablish rhythm in our
lives. The corridor is itself neutral, and every human being needs

neutral experiences in order to become receptive to the great discoveries that lie before us.

The corridor for Peter and his companions is the physical and mental concentration that makes up the nature of fishing. Added to that, the Sea of Galilee is the place where they had each spent so many years of their lives. Peter returned to the life-space pathways be understood best. Therefore, he would not have to figure out or remap the terrain as he would have to have done in a new place.

This return to a familiar lake with its shoreline provided the corridor effect the men needed. Galilee's Lake waters gave the crew a rest, but it was not itself the goal or real end of the voyage. The voyage in greater depths of a still greater sea has yet to confront the crew, but that voyage would be on another day. For now, the ship and its crew needed corridor time. As I see it, Peter was altogether wise to consciously and concretely move away from the intense and highly accelerated experiences of those powerful days after Easter toward the "time between times" space that the work of fishing provided.

There are people who in their earnest desire to be spiritually obedient have no understanding of this rhythmic principle of their own need for corridor experiences. These are persons who become exhausted because of unrelieved acceleration of activity and duty. They burn out because they are doing and talking and working all the time to exercise themselves in grace, but they are not listening and discovering the assurance of God's finding grace. Peter had run with John to the tomb on Easter morning. He was aggressive and powerful in that morning search; but now at Galilee he would be in a different stance, and it would be Jesus Christ himself who would search out the small crew and their ship. He would be the one who calls out to his friends, He would find Peter. "Lads, have you caught any fish?"

The fourth observation is that *Jesus asks Peter three questions that create a gospel barrier between present and past.*

John continues to tell the events of that morning to us.

> Just as day was breaking, Jesus stood on the beach; yet the disciples did not know that it was Jesus. Jesus said to them, "Children, have you any fish?" They answered him, "No." He said to them, "Cast the net on the right side of the boat, and you will find some." So they cast it, and now they were not able to haul it in, for the quantity of fish. That disciple whom Jesus loved said to Peter, "It is the Lord!" When Simon Peter heard that it was the Lord, he put on his clothes, for he was stripped for work, and sprang into the sea. But the other disciples came in the boat, dragging the net full of fish, for they were not far from the land, but about a hundred yards off.
>
> When they got out on land, they saw a charcoal fire there, with fish lying on it, and bread. Jesus said to them, "Bring some of the fish that you have just caught." So Simon Peter went aboard and hauled the net ashore, full of large fish, a hundred and fifty-three of them; and although there were so many, the net was not torn. Jesus said to them, "Come and have breakfast." Now none of the disciples dared ask him, "Who are you?" They knew it was the Lord. Jesus came and took the bread and gave it to them, and so with the fish. This was now the third time that Jesus was revealed to the disciples after he was raised from the dead.
>
> When they had finished breakfast, Jesus said to Simon Peter, "Simon, son of John, do you love me more than these?" He said to him, "Yes, Lord; you know that I love you." He said to him, "Feed my lambs." A second time he said to him, "Simon, son of John, do you love me?" He said to him, "Yes, Lord; you know that I love you." He said to him, "Tend my sheep." He said to him the third time, "Simon, son of John, do you love me?" Peter was grieved because he said to him the third time, "Do you love me?" And he said to him, "Lord, you know everything; you know that I love you." Jesus said to him, "Feed my sheep." (John 21:4-17)

Jesus' threefold questions of Peter have been much discussed but it seems to me as an interpreter of this very significant moment in the encounter of Peter with his Lord, that the obvious interpretation is the most helpful. Jesus asks three questions of Peter that inquire about his present conviction and each answer by Peter is followed by a future-tense great commission spoken by his Lord.

What has happened is that Jesus has created a threefold gospel barrier between Peter and the past. It is done in the most powerful way by the threefold present-tense questions, "Do you love me?" When Peter hears the third question he is grieved, probably because he now is forced to remember his threefold denial. But the grief is short-lived, and it is resolved in the only way interior doubt can be resolved—by the Lord who is able to forgive our real failures of the past.

This Redeemer Lord is also the only one able to place our feet in the vital present without the paralyzing effect of past failure to haunt us. He is Lord of the future, and Jesus Christ, by this encounter, carefully reestablishes Peter as the leader among the disciples' band. John's record makes this reestablishment clear.

These final stages in Peter's resolution amount to *his rediscovery of the good news* not only as the truth for others but also as the truth for himself. Once he understands that the gospel is for Peter, then—and only then—is he safe to be a servant leader in the mission of the church with his hands, but not before.

Peter is now able to help us all in our own journeys through his own experience of resolution of his internal doubt.

QUESTIONS FOR FURTHER STUDY

1. How do you feel people lose self-confidence? Why does that loss affect faith?

2. Are you intrigued by the threefold, present-tense questions of Jesus? How do these questions relate to internal doubt?

3. Can you offer a definition of faith for Peter that includes his total experience with Jesus Christ?

4. What is your definition of faith?

WHY BELIEVE?

There are so many reasons for believing in God. G. K. Chesterton, in the telling of his own pilgrimage, shows how he was prepared for faith in Jesus Christ long before he knew the Lord of the good news. He describes this yearning for the good news as five discoveries that had dawned upon him before he knew there was such a thing as good news:

> I felt in my bones, first, that this world does not explain itself . . . the thing is magic, true or false. Second, I came to feel as if magic must have a meaning, and meaning must have someone to mean it. There was something personal in the world, as in a work of art, whatever it meant it meant violently. Third, I thought this purpose beautiful in its old design, in spite of its defects, such as dragons. Fourth, the proper form of thanks to it is some form of humility and restraint; we should thank God for beer and burgundy by not drinking too much of them . . . and last, the strangest, there came into my mind a vague and vast impression that in some way all good was remnant to be stored and held sacred out of some primordial ruin . . . All this I felt and the age gave me no encouragement to feel it.[1]

I have this same feeling when I listen closely to many non-religious people as they express their intuitions and longings. They are being prepared for the Lord of the gospel by their intuitions. Jesus of Nazareth is the one who is the fulfillment of their hopes, and Redeemer of their crises.

Faith takes place when these yearnings meet the good news about the man Jesus Christ. As Pascal reminds us, "It is good to be weary and worn out in the vain pursuit of the true good so that we may open our arms to the Redeemer."

Faith takes place when Jesus Christ wins us to himself, so that we discover his lordship as directed toward us, and we hear his truth as reality.

His truth is the bedrock reality of all time. He is the Amen Rock who, like a fortress, stands through the storm. But faith is more than a fortress, it is more than hearing about the faithfulness of God. Faith is also profoundly rich in its emotional content. Faith happens when we meet Jesus Christ personally and when we trust his love as totally personal, so that we are able to relax because of that love.

When the moment of faith in Christ really happens it means that we wager on him and his character, even though all the evidence is not in and all the proofs are not complete. Karl Barth explained it well, we trust in the person Jesus Christ "in spite of all that contradicts." This "in spite of" is very important to preserve because we must not cancel out the fact that we are not cancelled out. The time between discovery and restoration is not taken away from us.

Faith must always be a grand improbability, a wonderful incongruity, because we are never fully ready and we are never personally worthy of so great a gift. Faith is the gift we receive and the gift we give. We receive it because God's love is prior to our faith. His faithfulness invites our trust, his confirmation makes faith possible because he must authenticate himself.

Faith is our gift to give because it is the most essential crisis of all crises in which I as a human being decide to trust in the one who stands in my place. It is the crisis in which I decide to trust his forgiveness, to put my weight down upon his love, and then to believe his promises.

We have seen how John the Baptist, Thomas and Peter made decisions to trust in God in despite their uncertainties and unanswered questions. On the basis of what you know about Jesus Christ, are you willing to trust his trustworthiness?

NOTES

CHAPTER 1

1. Some translations have followed several ancient manuscripts in reversing the order of the brothers. For example, the *New American Standard Bible* and *New English Bible* record that the first son said, "I will sir" and the second son, "I will not." The significance of the parable with each case remains the same. I have chosen the *NRSV* and most other translations in their presentation of the text because the oldest manuscript *Codex Sinaiticus* sides with this rendering.

2. C. S. Lewis, *Miracles* (New York: Macmillan, 1960), 131.

CHAPTER 2

1. *The Dictionary of the Old Testament* (Grand Rapids: Eerdmans), 322.

2. Gerhard von Rad, *Old Testament Theology, Vol. 1* (Trans. D. M. G. Stalker; New York: Harper & Row, 1962), 171.

3. I owe this "feet planted firmly in the air" saying to my friend and fellow pastor Rev. Frank Jackson. He was describing to me one day the way he felt about some of the bold pronouncements that we as church people

make about issues in which our statements are not founded upon biblical faith.

4. Karl Barth, *Dogmatics in Outline* (New York: Harper & Row, 1959), 15.

5. F. Dale Bruner, *Theology of the Holy Spirit* (Grand Rapids: Eerdmans, 1970), 318–319.

6. Helmut Theilicke, *Theological Ethics* (Philadelphia: Fortress Press, 1969), 3.

7. Ibid, 4.

CHAPTER 3

1. C. S. Lewis, *The Silver Chair* (New York: Macmillan, 1953), 15.

CHAPTER 4

1. Karl Barth describes the ministry of the Holy Spirit in these words in *Dogmatics in Outline.*

2. Blaise Pascal, *Pensées* (London: Penguin, 1966), 82.

CHAPTER 5

1. C. S. Lewis, *Screwtape Letters* (New York: Macmillan, 1961), 38–39.

CHAPTER 6

1. Blaise Pascal, *Pensées* (London: Penguin, 1966), 271.

2. C. S. Lewis, *Miracles* (New York: Macmillan, 1978), 109.

CHAPTER 7

1. C. S. Lewis, *Screwtape Letters* (New York: Macmillan, 1961), 115–116.

CHAPTER 8

1. Jon Palmer, "Job" (student paper, Stanford University, 1983), 4.

2. Ibid., p. 1

3. Ibid., p. 4.

4. Ibid., p. 3.

CHAPTER 11

1. John Updike, *Telephone Poles and Other Poems* (New York: Alfred A. Knopf, 1961).

POSTSCRIPT

1. G.K. Chesterton, *Orthodoxy* (New York: Dodd, Mead, & Co., 1916).

SUBJECT INDEX

John the Baptist
  baptism, 96
  belief in, 13–14, 17
  doubts, disappointments and
      demands, 78, 96, 98
  imprisonment, 97
  people's prophet, 94–96
  questions Jesus, 100–101
  reproves Herod, 97
  resolution of his doubt, 102
Johnson, Samuel, 85
Judaism
  tradition and ritual
  circumcision, 49–50, 64
  Sabbath keeping, 98, 100–101
justification, 48

K
kite flying, 68
kite poems
  "I am the Kite," 69–70
  "The Kite Tangled in the Tree," 70
  "I am the Balloon," 71
kite string tension, 69

L
legalism, 27, 48, 50, 66
Lewis, C.S., 17–18
  The Chronicles of Narnia, 85
  Miracles, 16, 60–61
  Screwtape Letters, 52, 67
  The Silver Chair, 36, 103
Lord of the Rings (JRR Tolkien), 94
Luke, 43, 65
Luther, Martin, 59

M
marriage, 31, 61
Martha, 78
Matthew, 75–77
Mears, Henrietta
  Forest Home Christian Conference
      Center
  Hollywood Presbyterian Church, 29
Miller, Arthur
  Death of a Salesman, 94
mountain climbing, 89–90

N
Nathanael, 86, 91
New College, Berkeley, 9
Nicodemus, 37
No Exit (Sartre), 87

P
Palmer, Jon
  study of Job, 77–78
parables
  flying kites, 68
  Kingdom parable, 15
  mustard seed, 15
  prodigal son, 36, 38
  two sons, 13–17, 35
Pascal, Blaise, 59, 61
  absolute proof, 54
  Pensées
  three observations about humanity, 46
  three reasons for faith, 57
  and yearnings, 124
Pasternak, Boris
  Dr. Zhivago, 98
Paul
  call to present ourselves, 38
  on circumcision, 49–50
  encounter with Peter at Antioch,
      47–48
  and faith, 26, 51, 59
  letter to the Romans, 105
  letter to the Thessalonians, 43
  putting his weight on Jesus Christ, 48
  warning, 66–67
  and works, 63–64
Peter, 42
  denies Jesus, 115
  and doubt, 114–118
  encounter with Paul at Antioch, 47–48
  fishing, 118–120
  Jesus' three questions, 120–121
  resolution of doubt, 121
Pharisees, 98
Pippert, Becky Manley, 99
Plato, 27
pornography, 87
Post-modern Christian existential
      philosophy, 30
putting down weight on faithfulness of
      God, 25, 29, 44, 48, 62, 125

R
repentance, 16, 64
resurrection
   See Jesus Christ, resurrection

S
Sartre, Jean Paul
   No Exit, 87
   Words, 88
scientific enquiry, 46
Sea of Galilee. *See* Galilee
shama. *See* faith
Shoemaker, Sam, Reverend of Pittsburgh,
   51
Simon. *See* Peter
skepticism, 86
"Such a Windy Place," 11

T
Taylor, Hudson
   Overseas Missionary Fellowship, 28
Thielicke, Helmut
   Barmen Declaration, 30–31

Theological Ethics, 30
Thomas, 106, 110–111
Tillich, Paul, 30–31
Tolstoy, Leo
   War and Peace, 20
trust, 17–18, 26, 29, 38, 42
truth, 72, 111
truthfulness, 23–24, 37, 41–42, 44–46, 49
twenty-first century issues, 110

U
University of California, Berkeley, 19, 44
University Presbyterian Church
   Seattle, Washington, 53, 69
Updike, John
   Couples, 94, 98
   "Seven Stanzas at Easter," 110–111

W
works, 63–64

SCRIPTURE INDEX

Printed in the United States
76673LV00004B/79-105